# Studies in American Literature

*Editor by*
Mohit K. Ray

ATLANTIC
PUBLISHERS & DISTRIBUTORS (P) LTD

Published by
**ATLANTIC**
PUBLISHERS & DISTRIBUTORS (P) LTD
7/22, Ansari Road, Darya Ganj,
New Delhi-110002
Phones : +91-11-40775252, 23273880, 23275880, 23280451
Fax : +91-11-23285873
Web : www.atlanticbooks.com
E-mail : orders@atlanticbooks.com

Branch Office
5, Nallathambi Street, Wallajah Road,
Chennai-600002
Phones : +91-44-64611085, 32413319
E-mail : chennai@atlanticbooks.com



Printed in India at Nice Printing Press, A-33/3A, Site-IV, Industrial Area, Sahibabad, Ghaziabad, U.P.

# PREFACE

In this volume we start discussions with the American tradition of poetry as reflected in and enriched by the poetry of Robert Frost. Then moving through Tennessee Williams, Arthur Miller, Sylvia Plath and Philip Roth we finally focus on Ernest Hemingway.

Seven highly perceptive studies by eminent scholars on different aspects of Hemingway offer substantial meat as much for Hemingway scholars as for anybody interested in this great Nobel Laureate of keen active interest in the celebration of life in diverse ways.

Gajendra Kumar evaluates the contribution of Robert Frost to the tradition of American poetry.

Vinod K. Maheshwari shows how in Tennessee Williams' plays the sense of alienation arising out of different kinds of conflict is ultimately resolved in a note of affirmation.

In Gunjan Agarwal's study of Arthur Miller's handling of the problem of guilt his protagonists emerge as tragic heroes who sacrifice their lives for their families.

N.B. Masal highlights the points of affinity between Sylvia Plath's novel *The Bell Jar* and her short story, "Tongues of Stone."

C.C. Mishra argues convincingly that Philip Roth's critique of American philistinism makes room for the possibility of a new order.

In her well-researched paper Susheela Beniwal builds up her arguments almost brick by brick to correct the wrong notion that Hemingway reduces his female characters to mere props, and shows how Hemingway really puts women on a plane of equality with men.

Taking cue from Hemingway's reference to *Nada* (a Spanish word that means 'nothing/nothingness') Mary Mohanty shows how the material defeat is transmuted into a spiritual and moral triumph for a Hemingway protagonist.

Rama Kundu makes a fine Bloom-ian study of Hemingway's *The Torrents of Spring,* an early work, and shows how a close reading of the novel gives us an idea of a great artist in the making, struggling to get over the influence of his illustrious predecessor.

Ishteyaque Shams has made an indepth study of the symbols, both universal and innovative, and various images that contribute to the substance and quality of Hardy's vision, particularly in *The Sun Also Rises.*

Amiya K. Patra has examined three major novels of Hemingway to show how the heroes arrive at ultimate victory — moral and metaphysical — after going through intense suffering, endurance and love.

From a different perspective Gajendra Kumar also tries to establish how the novel *The Old Man and the Sea* records a journey from the social life to natural life, and how Santiago's heroic struggle with destiny ensures his moral triumph.

Mohit K. Ray tries to show how the novel *The Old Man and the Sea* is built around the archetypal theme of the hunter and the hunt.

Anybody who is interested in American Literature will find this book extremely interesting. Teachers, scholars and students of American Literature will also find the book useful because of the authors' masterly handling of some of the major American writers and texts of the past century.

I thank all the contributors to this volume for their well-researched papers.

I also thank my colleague Professor Rama Kundu for valuable assistance.

My special thanks go to Dr. K.R. Gupta, Managing Director, M/s Atlantic Publishers and Distributors, New Delhi for the confidence evinced in me, and for seeing the book through the press.

**MOHIT K. RAY**
*Editor*

# CONTENTS

# 1

# The American Tradition of Poetry and Robert Frost

*—Gajendra Kumar*

IN THE comprehensive critical historiography of American literature from the seventeenth century to the modern age, poetry has ever been the attention arresting area. Theoretically it has been pinpointed that the literary personages and critics have been conscious not of the history of the creating poems but rather with the history which poems have created. To Ezra Pound, "Literature is news which stays news." But literary news has always been the news of culture and ethos. In the historical framework, the achievement of American poetry is based upon the achievement of American culture as a whole. The poetry itself is a sensitive study of the poet's particular relation to his culture in order to explore the best possible use of the language which establishes him at the centre.

The poet by sitting at the centre of culture tries to seek or search communications where he adds phenomenal features to the styles and spirit. The poet constantly but critically inquires into the genuineness and comprehensiveness of that style and spirit. The American poets have ever been considered conservatives usually very eclectic in their attitude and articulation as to appear to be revolutionaries conservatives. While they are making an effort to clinch at work, their explorations of language have enabled the readers to understand the nature of challenges and threats for the survival and the regular growth of the poetic imagination and sensibility. Their tradition of literature, the tradition their literature makes critically manifests their perennial heroic contribution on the margin of the American sensibility, yet plunging directly to its vital centre. The 'Americanness' is the principal concern and commitment of American poetry which is characterised as its compulsive modernism or more particularly in the twentieth century, a professed form of modernism. Poems like men have their own existence only in this universe. In this poetic cosmos, we come across a cultural behaviour of a poet's age against which the poetic mind writes, grows and becomes the epoch-making voice of the contemporary ethos. My sole intention is to expound, interpret and appreciate the achievement of Robert Frost in the tradition of American poetry and to examine those basic intrinsic values and views whose continuity constitutes its growth and grandeur.

In the annal of the twentieth century American poetry, Robert Frost appears to be the unofficial poet laureate. He is credited to get two covetous prizes from Oxford and Cambridge in the same year 1957, an honour previously given only to two other American poets Longfellow in 1868 and James Russell Lowell in 1873. He had his own reasons to respect England as his mother country. It is proved to be the fertile place where the poetic sensibility grew in him. He was profoundly under the charm and spell of Milton from whom he derived that sonorous sense of the mythological dimensions of conjugal love that echo in one of his brilliant — sonnets, "Never Again Would Bird's Song Be the Same," and in the marital tensions of his long narrative — dramatic poems, like "Home Burial." In the poetic world of Spenser and Keats, he locates tropes for such melodious song like poems of mutability as "Spring Pools." Here we can have voices of Pope's early pastorals in "A Prayer in Spring" of Marvell's mower poems in the great sonnet "Mowing", of Dante Gabriel Rossetti's "The Wood Spurge" in "The Vantage Point." His tastes were wide ranging and eclectic. In the prime of his youth, he wrote to Susan Hayes Ward who had consented to publish his first poem, "My Butterfly," that his favourite poems are and have been these : Keats's "Hyperion," Shelley's "Prometheus," Tennyson's "Morte D'Arthur" and Browning's "Saul" — all of them about the giants (Letters 20).

England was considered to be the mother country even from another point of view. Actually, it was not in America that Frost's poetic career had its real start. In England he succeeded to meet Ezra Pound, Yeats and a number of poets who contributed for an anthology called Georgian Poetry. He came into contact with the recently appointed poet laureate Robert Bridges, who became a great admirer and lover of Frost's poetry and who until his death was probably the most beloved and trustworthy friend of his life. In England he wrote several poems : first a collection of lyrics entitled *A Boy's Will* published in England in 1913, and a second, the collection of dramatic narrative poems called *North of Boston* came out in 1914. He had sufficient poetic materials for his next book *Mountain Interval* which appeared in 1916 after his coming back to the United States. Both the early books were very remarkably reviewed and responded by new admirers like Pound, F.S. Flint, Gibson, Abercrombie and most perceptively by Edward Thomas who reviewed *North of Boston.* During this period, through his letters Frost had demonstrated his agony and anxiety as T.S. Eliot showed his desire to enthuse critics and artists to observe the historical significance and originality of his poetic nuances and finesse.

Frost, from beginning to the end, was sincerely devoted to the shaping and moulding of a poetic career; rather he was well decided to prove his mettle among the American poetic talents. His sonnets are analysed as the best ever written in American poetry which has included variations in the very syntactic structure of the lines. He created two masques : *A Masque of Reason* and *A Masque of Mercy.* He discovered occasional epigrams, one of which entitled "From Iron," is structurally phenomenal having complex views : "Nature within her inmost self divides/To trouble men with having to take sides." Through his great dramatic-narrative poems in which the monologue

"Mending Wall" is a noted illustration, he declared that he had "dropped to an everyday level of diction that even Wordsworth kept above" (Letters 83-84). T.S. Eliot in his moving attributes to Frost during a dinner organised in his honour in London in 1957 remarks :

> "Mr. Frost is one of the good poets, and I might say, perhaps the most eminent, the most distinguished, I must call it, Anglo-American poet now living. I have a special weakness, perhaps — no, I should not call it a weakness — I have a special understanding of a great deal of his work. Of course, I also have the New England background. But I think that there are two kinds of local feeling in poetry. There is one kind which makes that poetry only accessible to people who had the same background to whom it means a great deal. And there is another kind that can go with universality : the relation of Dante to Florence, of Shakespeare to Warwickshire, of Goethe to the Rhineland, the relation of Robert Frost to New England" (Thomson and Winnick, 243).

This is wonderfully elevating and affecting tribute from one great soul to another because throughout Eliot and Frost did not maintain a rapport which could be termed as very amiable or very admiring. At the same time we witness a group of poets and thinkers like Emerson, William James, Frost and Stevens who plead for skepticism and modernist theoretical formulations so overwhelming as to anticipate later theorising and philosophing the deconstructive tendencies of language. In the critical scrutiny, Frost's intimate attachment with Emerson and William James finds a literary manifestation when all the three simultaneously aspire to be popular. At once, Frost did not get recognition, he earned name and fame solely because of Eliot's efforts. Frost's authenticity consists largely in his subversions of accredited ideas of what it means to be serious to "get credit for thinking." In the Jamesian manner, he does not reject the notion of God or Truth. He simply combines such terms with more simpler or lesser ones, and by changing voice and vision and metaphor tests their endurance. The minute details of his imaginative faculty are meant for revealing, determining and positioning the poetic canon what might be significant. Frost very categorically deals with the meaning of the word in a Wordsworthian manner and suggests that meaning is meaning which is meant by the general people in their everyday life. Frost firmly believed that a poet must stand true to the test of time and people. He points out that "really to arrive where I can stand on my legs as a poet and nothing else I must get outside that circle to the general reader.... I want to be a poet for all sorts and kinds" (Letters 98).

Frost had arranged his first meeting with Edward Thomas just a month earlier while Thomas's review of *A Boy's Will* came out. Thomas's grudge against Pound came up which was directed not at what he was doing rather how it might be feasible to advocate in poetry without being poetic. In fact he was locating, inventing and trying to codify another kind of aloofness for the language of poetry. Frost got us involved in the most subtle and sustainable kinds of poetic voice against the patterned use of meter where resonances of earlier poetry are casually allowed to mingle with the sounds of common speech. Transparency is not the only phenomenal feature of great poetry rather it demands, strenuous effort if the people are to divest themselves. The rhythmic patterns in a poem can create, correct and sustain a community of effort where the writer and the reader might locate and decode ideal versions of themselves which can be visualised in life.

Like Wordsworth, Frost champions the power of poetry which can make or mould possibilities in the sense that modernist nature of poetic difficulty can be amended. Poetry explores language in order to discover those possibilities for community of feeling with which we have only the most occasional contact. The poet has to search out a common or general reader in the benefit of some wider cultural or spiritual quest. The poets in modern civilisational set up are bound to be tough because of the complex nature of society. The modern civilisation comprehends great variety and complexity and, no doubt, this variety and complexity are influencing the refined sensibility. The poet must make an effort to be more and more comprehensive, more allusive, more indirect in order to pursue, to dislocate and to decode the meaningful dimensions of language philosophy. While Eliot was engrossed in 'The Waste Land' for its publication, it was the crucial time for him to propose and propound that kind of 'difficulty', 'allusiveness', 'complexity' and 'dislocation' which are more or less a direct literary outcome of some unprecedented cultural-historical crisis. Frost as a sensitive poet became increasingly acquainted in the 1930s with the most of the poetic elements.

Frost was keenly intelligent about literary and cultural politics to find himself as a public alternative to Eliot or to Eliot's modernism more especially in an American literary situation. There he might then locate himself in the rich associations of Vachel Lindsay, Edgar Lee Masters and Carl Sandbury. The very marked difference from Eliot came to focus when Frost remarked "He is a pessimistic Christian, I'm an optimistic pagan." Really, it was William Carles not Frost who decided to enunciate an 'American' difference from Eliot on the ground of 'Local conditions' and who exemplifies the unrewarding feature of the distinction. Frost was highly choosy in his nature and character. He chose a title 'The Figure a Poem Makes' in 1939, for the preface of his *Collected Poems* incorporating Emersonian theories in the face of any idea of a static poetic meaning ultimately searched out. In his critical assertion, he believes that poems should be always made for the proper causes, needs and the creators should for a moment stay against confusion. These concluding remarks signify the literary spirit of Robert Frost which have been taken from his "The Figure a Poem Makes." He is the singular modern American poet of repute who was not found unnecessarily in a fix by the fact. In his critical assessment of his whole career, Frost has expressed his desire to define :

"I owe more to Emerson than anyone else for troubled thoughts about freedom. I had the hurt to get over when I first heard us made fun of by foreigners as the land of the free and the home of the brave. Haven't we won freedom? Is there no such thing as freedom? Well, Emerson says of God :

> Would take the Sun out of the skies
> Ere freedom out of a man.

and there rings the freedom I choose.... I am on record as saying that freedom is nothing but departure — setting forth — leaving things behind, brave origination of the courage to be new...."

("On Emerson", *Daedalus* : *Proceedings of the American Academy,* LXXXVIII (1959), 715.)

It is worthwhile to note that Frost allies himself with Emerson not Whitman. This way he suggests that he has turned down the temptation to take a path of poetry which only a person as tremendous as Whitman could take without losing his identity as poet. Frost was aware of the dangerous consequences of the much inwardness ever better than Emerson. No doubt this is an Emersonian philosophy. Frost is a poet of hard-headed nature having self-reliance, village style and a poet of sound. Frost has no taste to emerge as a 'contemporary' poet for which Emerson was inclined to be. Frost being a poet thoroughly understood himself and he has a good record of exacting details. He did not ever relish philosophy of self or inwardness. Here we come across the loss of inclusiveness and the posture of everwidening possibility which are characterised as Emersonian features. Frost at his best manifests the poetic mannerism of Emerson to imitate it in his own way and to make it a means so that a certain stability and certitude might be achieved. As a poet he does not resemble a political leader rather he wants to emerge as culture hero. Before the poetic era of Frost the literary spectrum of American poetry was narrow. Being a poet, he acknowledges his limitations against which he worked and achieved excellences. In his poetic imagination he presents a cosmos in which he was very much there. He has selected a title for one of his late poems, that is eye catching. The title of the poem is "Not quite Social." In this poem, the poet says :

> "Some of you will be glad I did what I did,
> And the rest won't want to punish me too severely —

For finding a thing to do that though not forbid
Yet wasn't enjoined and wasn't expected clearly."

The conditions which describe Frost's poem are those of universe which was not yet dominated by urban, industrialised, bureaucratised culture. Frost's glance at this world is merely a venture for better understanding. Frost's world focuses on proper life style which generates the literary style and underlines the significance of Frost. Frost's protagonists seem to be unsocialised because they do not enjoy this modern world and they are also least concerned with the transformations. Frost's literary output, at last, comes as a series of expressions of that refusal and assessment of its cost. The cost is great, and is acknowledged unflinchingly. His individualism, as it is manifested in his works is of a self which is emphatically liberated to express the savage tinge over the roof tops of the world. He articulates one of the most telling expressions in his late poem "Directive" :

"Back out of all this now too much for us,
Back in a time made simple by the loss
Of detail, burned, dissolved, and broken off
Like graveyard marble sculpture in the weather."

The opening statement is marked first by a groping hesitant syntax, then by a series of strong parallelisms; a shifting accent reinforces the shifting syntactic effect. Therefore the poet hesitates and then confronts the modern universe. Afterwards as he plans to describe the place, he finds a place, however foregone, to describe the tone and tenor. And his accents are regular consisting in the effect-orientated achievement by the parallelisms. The house and its "village culture" are lost to him. He tells the reader :

"And if you're lost enough to find yourself
By now, pull in your ladder road behind you
And put a sign up CLOSED to all but me
Then make yourself at home."

Frost is quite different from Emerson in "Each and All" and says :

"I yielded myself to the perfect whole."
He is very akin to Melville's
Bartleby, with his "I prefer not to."

Bartleby was driven to prison and suicide. Frost is led forward to mountain and farm to wholeness "beyond confusion." His philosophy of self-assertion is an act performed in a place that is not at all a place and in a time that is no longer a time but a memory of one. In one of his earliest poems, "The Vantage Point" he argues :

"If tired of trees I seek again mankind,
Well I know where to hie me — in the dawn,
To a slope where the cattle keep the lawn.
There amid Lolling Juniper reclined,
Myself unseen, I see in white defined
Far off the homes of men..."

There stands a confusion but from a certain distance. The distance is as such that the poet could not listen to us even if we did know how to speak back to him. But we have had the philosophy of organic 'wholeness' and have been brought to acknowledge the fact that each man's concept of wholeness is his own. All he aspires for the writer is "freedom." The poet asserts :

"Political freedom is nothing to me.

I bestow it right and left. All I would keep for myself is the freedom of my material — the condition of body and mind now and then to summons aptly from the vast chaos of all I have lived through."

The poet, simply enough, wants to be free to be himself. And later : "The artist must value himself as he snatches a thing from some previous order in time and space into a new order with not so much as a ligature clinching to it of the old place where it was organic."

Frost is inclined to have a new order which is the product of a recovery and reconstitution rather than reinvention and transformation of the old. The leading 19th century poets believe that life meaningfully stands for an infinite series of willed, self-generated transformations forward. According to the poetic theory of Frost, transformation opportunity gives us a stabilising point where it does not lead towards advancement but of withdrawal and consolidation. Frost has considered freedom as departure. But as soon as he departs, he looks backward not forward. Frost's representative poems remarkably underline his certainty that he is one kind of man moving down one kind of road. Some of his poems are monologues and dialogues which began in *North of Boston* early in his career. Repeatedly the subject of the poem is failure of communication, a failure which shows how small and delimited the effective community can be.

It is very much obvious that all men of greater sensibility who relish it will come to focus that they can communicate only the fact that they cannot communicate and they can discover the limited terms in which they can communicate this fact. Frost always keeps a desire to go behind something. He always comes across a failure and there is the triumph to live with it and to discover the condition of strength because here lies the strength in discovering oneself as a person. In the dramatic poems the realisations are not meant for the protagonists rather for the poets as a result of the total effect of the poem. In this kind of deliberation, Robert Frost seems to be more a novelist than a poet because of the intimate analysis of the conditions of the particular kinds of failures. No doubt, we often find the moments of pure, unmediated realisation, however — epiphanies. These moments are defined privately in first — person lyrics for example, "Tree at My Window", "Desert Places", "The Tuft of Flowers", "The Road Not Taken", "Bereft", "Once by the Pacific", "Stopping by Woods" and so many other poems.

Frost makes us sure that the failure is inevitable and therefore it becomes a means or matrix of making some sort of decision regarding the nature of his world, its people and their meaning for us. He is more than a realist who delights everybody in his realism to confirm that many of his readers will not be in a position to imitate him intimately. Hence in his later poetry, "Lesson For Today" he finally finds the malaise and justifies his approach :

"Space ails us moderns : we are sick with space.
Its contemplation makes us out as small
As a brief epidemic of microbes
That in a good glass may be seen to crawl
The patina of this the least of globes."

But he does believe that "one age is like another for the soul." He says :

"We all are doomed to broken-off careers,
And so's the nation, so's the total race.
The earth itself is liable to the fate
Of meaninglessly being broken off."

"I take my incompleteness with the rest.
God bless himself can no one else be blessed."

His powerful portrayal of the effectiveness, a sense of local detail is so fully controlled and commanded that it gives us the understanding of his world and all others. In a nutshell, it can be suggested that Robert Frost wonderfully fuses the sense of wholeness and individual sensibility :

"He thought he kept the universe alone;
For all the voice in answer he could wake
Was but the mocking echo of his own
From some tree-hidden cliff across the lake.
Some morning from the boulder-broken beach
He would cry out on life, that what it wants
Is not its own love back in copy speech,
But counter-love, original response.
And nothing ever came of what he cried
Unless it was the embodiment that crashed
In the cliff's talus on the other side,
And then in the far distant water splashed,
But after a time allowed for it to swim,
Instead of proving human when it neared
And someone additional to him,
As a great buck it powerfully appeared,
Pushing the crumpled water up ahead,
And landed pouring like a waterfall,
And stumbled through the rocks with
And forced the underbrush — and that was all."

Frost's "The Most of It" deals with the place and the occasion which opens the vistas of the hope that the protagonist is not really alone rather he keeps ambiguous sense. There lies the responsibility in between the setting and the poet-protagonist. It is the expression of a man who doubts even the echo of his own voice. Though at the end, the poet-protagonist certainly does not keep the "Universe alone", yet he cannot be said to "share it with the buck." Being a 'natural' as opposed to a 'human' universe, it is neither to be kept or shared. This is one of Frost's major subjects in a poem ranging from "Stopping by woods..." to "After Apple Picking." The poet is satisfied because he found what he sought. The occasion is not the means of "symbolising the poet's intimacy with nature." The poet locates the limit that he cannot go beyond it.

Frost in his considerate opinion presents the mountain world as farm world which is also an analogising occasion for inner direction. The poet cannot submit himself to the natural world. This is the sum total of his humanity, so, he turns inward toward the 'human'. Indubitably, this is man's universe. Society does not exist as an immediately conditioning factor in Frost's poetic universe. To him the other man is in effect part of the 'natural' world to which he must not yield. Frost has demonstrated his choice. He opens the option for himself and his protagonists like to choose, whereas Emerson liked himself to be chosen. Frost has always emphasised this point where he wants to move. His people do not suffer from agony and tormentation because they think that they have missed the possibilities. Frost makes his people conscious of their past. Hence the poet says in "New Hampshire" :

> "The glorious bards of Massachusetts seem
> To want to make New Hampshire people over
> They taunt the lofty land with little men.
> I don't know what to say about the people.
> For art's sake one could almost with them worse
> Rather than better. How are we to write
> The Russian novel in America
> As long as life goes so unterribly?

And later in the same poem :

> Lately in converse with a New York alec
> About the new school of the pseudo-phallic,
> I found myself in a close corner where
> I had to make an almost funny choice.
> Choose you which you will be — a prude or puke,
> Mewling and puking in the public arms.
> Me for the hills where I don't have to choose."

In a dramatic move Frost has presented a strategic deal by withdrawing himself from the viewpoint of a city couple to the country. They have their own suspicions about the wisdom of the move, and when the movers have left, the husband remarks :

> "...We puzzle them. They think —
> I don't know what they think we see in what
> They leave us to...."

Both the wife and husband are much tormented as to who first had the thought of moving out of the city. Theoretically, is this the beginning? the middle? the end? These are the husband's questions. The wife has had the courage to argue, "Ends and beginnings — there are no such things/There are only middles." In this poem, Frost's urban reader emerges as his protagonist and comes to learn that he may be able to formulate clear and coherent questionnaire. Frost gives a clear message to the urban reader that the condition of survival is a strategic withdrawal. The tone of withdrawal in Frost is intensified in the usually anti-political poems which he began to write after the publication of "New Hampshire" in 1923. It comes to the final form in the *Wry Masque of Reason* and *Masque of Mercy*, published in 1945 and 1947. Frost has come to taunt his reader, not to challenge him as he had done formerly. The comparative account clarifies that the English poets have abundant wit and a common sense but little imagination. Frost's earlier work reveals a glaring weakness, a weakness of character — "a cultivated willingness to be a thought — diver for himself and his kind." The two Masques, then are apologies for Frost's way with the American imagination. The poet remarks :

"We have lacked the courage in the heart
To overcome the fear within the soul
And go ahead to any accomplishment.
Courage is what it takes and takes the most of
Because the deeper fear is so eternal."

In the perspective of these things absolute satisfaction is not achieved. There exists the down-to-earth, philosophising of the Masques — this remarkably reflects the poetic calibre and sensitivity of the poet. To Emerson and others, life's journey is terrible and glorious. Frost candidly explicates that literary culture is necessarily political because it is either shaped by "the metaphor in vogue" or by resistance to it. To Frost, style provides ample evidence of how a person manages not to surrender himself to any mere idea. His style is a literary canon through which he carries himself towards his ideas. He strives for at least the effect of "modesty" in himself. This is a stylistic deliberation of language in his poetic output. He concedes this fact that the role of language is vital in poetry which enlightens the poetic imagination and sensibility. Like Emerson and Stevens, Frost is considered to be the least translatable of writers. He is committed to what William James misconstrued to underline his easy accommodation to the bourgeoise ethos, oftenly calls 'the cash value' of an idea, a conception or a word. Frost's letters moulded a new kind of human community or conversation which bears an intimate resemblance stylistically to the letters and lectures of William James.

Although Robert Frost tried to locate himself in the Emersonian tradition yet nothing can be transmitted with certitude. Even then critics seem to believe that Frost knows the answer of this million dollar question where and who he is. But more and more he has chosen to speak only to himself albeit in public. In his thoughtful manifestation Frost has renounced the nineteenth century belief that 'I' and 'We' connote the sense and spirit of equivalence. As a connoisseur of literature he does not go behind, unnecessarily, after the fact transcendentalism. His poetic achievement is concrete and somehow, is bounded by the sense of 'I' what Emily Dickinson has anticipated in her literary commitment. Marginally, Frost lacks the variety of Dickinson and her mind and capacious dimension.

## WORKS CITED

Bromwich, David, "Edward Thomas and Modernism," *Ravitan Quarterly,* 3 (Summer 1983) : 101-23.

Cook, Reginald, *Robert Frost : A Living Voice* (Amherst : University of Massachusetts Press, 1974), Part Two, pp. 29-195.

Cox, James M., (ed.), *Robert Frost : A Collection of Critical Essays* (Englewood Cliffs, N.J. Prentice Hall Inc, 1962).

Davie, Donald, *Ezra Pound* (New York : Viking Press, 1975).

Frost, Robert, *The Letters of Robert Frost to Lonis Untermeyer* (New York : Holt, Rinehart and Winston, 1963).

James, William, *The Meaning of Truth* (Cambridge : Harward University Press, 1982) — The Principles of Psychology (Cambridge : Harvard University Press, 1983).

Pearce, Roy Harvey, *The Continuity of American Poetry,* Princeton University Press, New Jersey, 1961.

Stevens, Wallace, *The Collected Poems,* (New York : Alfred A. Knoff, 1954).

Williams, William Carlos, *The Autobiography of William Carlos Williams* (New York : Random House, 1951).

Vendler Helen, (ed.), *Voices and Vision,* Tata McGraw-Hill Publishing Co. Ltd., New Delhi, 1989.

# 2

# Dehumanizing Forces in Modern Civilization : A Study of Alienation and Affirmation in *The Glass Menagerie* and *A Streetcar Named Desire*

*—Vinod Kumar Maheshwari*

ON GOING through his *Memoirs*[1] and biographical details of Tennessee Williams, provided by his contemporaries and interviewers, one comes to know that this great playwright was a man of great versatility in the sense that if he was concerned with the poor, he was equally capable of fidelity and devotion to his friends, for by virtue of his poetic sensibility, he reflected on the wonder and mystery of the human condition. From this background, it is possible to infer that if Williams unveiled the dark corridors of human life, he also showed the brighter side of life's panorama. Even as he was deeply upset over the social exploitation which caused alienation on personal, individual and social levels, he was equally elated by human potentialities in stemming the tide of darkness. In simple words, it means that he also believed in affirmation of life while being absorbingly concerned at the increase in dehumanizing forces in modern civilization.

In general, man's alienation arises when a living human being is besieged with forces — specially the social ones — hostile to his basic interests in terms of his survival and growth. Tennessee Williams has done a yeoman's job in transcribing the complicated facets of American life in legible terms. He understood the nature of American reality, which finds due expression in his plays. Since he was gifted with a poetic sensibility, he has put into perspective modern life through choice situations and select characters. Because of his poetic sensibility, he was able to telescope time — past, present and future — into one whole dynamic equilibrium, and it has enabled him to write his plays with a vision of life. As a consequence, he has been able to create viable characters who, in spite of their being alienated, resist the inroads of exploitation and social perversity and obscurantism. In this way, they affirm their life and destiny.

From his major plays : *The Glass Menagerie* (1944), *Summer and Smoke* (1947), *A Sreetcar Named Desire* (1947), *The Rose Tattoo* (1951), *Camino Real* (1953), *Cat on a Hot Tin Roof* (1955), *Orpheus Descending* (1957), *Sweet Bird of Youth* (1959) and *The Night of the Iguana* (1961), one can ferret out optimistic notes in the life style of different characters even as they are through the thick and thin of the ordeals of life. Being a gifted oblate at the shrine of the deepened life, Tennessee Williams covered a wide-ranging aspects of social and personal life, such as 'Nymphomania, promiscuity, rape, greed, alcoholism, impotence, homo-sexuality, profligacy, frigidity, crib fetishism, pedophilia, blowtorch killing, castration and dope addiction' among several other aberrations afflicting modern society; and yet, he has been able to touch upon the tender side of human life though such female characters as Amanda and Laura Wingfield (*The Glass Menagerie*), Alma Winemuller (*Summer and Smoke*), Blanche DuBois (*A Streetcar Named Desire*), Serefina delle Rose (*The Rose Tattoo*), Vee Talbot and Carol Cutrere (*Orpheus Descending*) and Hannah Jelkes (*The Night of the Iguana*).

It all shows that Williams was all along conscious of the brighter and darker sides of life. In most of his major plays the tone and tenor of the dramatic process is conducted from a positively higher point of view. For example, if one cares to go through *The Glass Menagerie,* one would find that Amanda

Wingfield as mother possessed a positive outlook towards her son and daughter. Having been estranged from her husband, Amanda cared for her two children. She was very much interested that her son, Tom Wingfield should grow into a healthy boy, bodily and mentally both. In scene 3, one finds, Amanda advising her son, Tom Winglfield not to read books which may defile his mind. In her opinion, Lawrence was an insane writer and so, her son should not read him : "I cannot control the output of diseased minds or people who cater to them" (*CAAL* 1853).

As she was interested in the overall well-being of her son, Tom Wingfield, she saw to it that he grows on right lines. Precisely, she had advised him to avoid reading befouled literature. She may have erred in misunderstanding Lawrence; but what is to be appreciated is her concern for the growth and development of her son. When she came to know that Tom goes to the movies quite often, she tried to wean him away from such a bad practice : "Nobody goes to the movies at nearly midnight, ...Come in stumbling. Muttering to yourself like a maniac. You get three hours' sleep and then to work. Oh! I can picture the way you're doing down there. Moping doping, because you're in no condition" (1854).

Amanda showed her motherly interest in Tom in different ways. She was acutely conscious that life's subtle texture is woven by the inter playing of many little things. On one occasion, she advised him to know what is the best way of eating one's meals : "*Amanda* (to her son)...If you have to push with something, the thing to push with is a crust of bread. And chew-chew! Animals have secretions in their stomachs which enable them to digest food without mastication, but human beings are supposed to chew their food before they swallow it down. Eat food leisurely, son, and really enjoy it. A well cooked meal has lots of delicate that have to be held in the mouth. So chew your food and give your salivary glands a chance to function" (1847). Then, she told her son not to smoke too much. Like this, she tried to tone up the life-attitude of her son.

Since the subject of 'gentlemen callers' was in the air, Amanda as mother found it appropriate to tell her son and daughter about the behaviour of the gentlemen callers in her own days in the south. To her inquisitive son inquiring about the nature of talks she used to have with them, Amanda told : "Things of importance going on in the world. Never anything coarse or common or vulgar.... My callers were gentleman...." (1848). It makes it very plain that Amanda tried to install in her son a taste for culture. It does show her affirmative attitude towards life.

Tennessee Williams has also brought into focus in a dramatic manner the hurt feelings of Amanda after her having known from the typing instructor at Rubicam's Business College — where her daughter, Laura Wingfield was supposed to have enrolled for learning typing — that she was not attending the college since January. At first the instructor showed complete ignorance about Laura's attending the college; but on being pressed again and again by Amanda, the typing instructor tried to identify the girl, saying : "I wonder, if you could be talking about that terribly shy little girl who dropped out of school after only a few days attendance" (1850). Amanda must have felt consternated on knowing all this about her daughter not attending the training institute. In the extract being cited below, Williams has given a graphic picture of the shock and dismay she had felt on her daughter's playing truancy from the college.

Precisely, when her daughter inquired of her mother how the D.A.R. (Daughters of American Revolution) was, she in agitation exclaimed "Deception? Deception?" and on being queried if she had gone to the D.A.R. meeting, Amanda spoke with a subdued sense of disappointment : "No. No..... I did not have the strength — to go to the D.A.R. In fact, I did not have the courage. I wanted to find a hole in the ground and hide myself in it forever" (1849). Apparently, sensing that her mother has faced something unusual, Laura with a sense of trepidation queried : why she had removed the diagram of the typewriter keyboard on the wall, and why she had torn it into two pieces after staring at it sweetly and sorrowfully; and when she found her mother repeating the performance now with the chart of the Gregg Alphabet, she endearingly put it "Why are you...." Then Amanda quizzically parried : "Why? Why? How old are you, Laura?"

Laura : Mother, you know my age.

Amanda : I Thought you were an adult; it seems that I was mistaken. (She crosses slowly to the sofa and sinks down and stares at Laura.) ...What are we going to do? What is going to become of us, what the future? (1849)

Amanda's main point in adopting a circuitous mode of conversation with Laura was first to create an aura of tragic seriousness; and then, to make her daughter aware about the serious lapse she had committed in not going to the typing institute. Amanda's playing on a near-tragic note was intended only to make her daughter aware of the intensity of her feelings for daughter's future welfare. Her bewilderment and shock at her daughter's in not learning typing arose out of her deep concern for Laura's betterment. Psychologically and culturally, Amanda desired intensely that her daughter should be well placed in life. When she told Laura that those girls who are not able to carve a business career, they usually get married to some nice men and that her daughter should follow this prescription, "Laura (*in a tone of frightened apology*) said : I'm crippled." In an admonishing tone, Amanda commented : "Nonsense! Laura, I've told you never, never to use that word. Why, you're not crippled, you just have a little defect — hardly noticeable, even when people have some slight disadvantage like that, they cultivate other things to make up for it — develop charm — and vivacity — and — charm. That's all you have to do.... One thing your father had plenty of — was charm" (1852).

All these extracts very well testify that Williams created characters like Amanda who fought against the odds and looked forward for a better future for children. It all shows interest in life in a positive manner. To remain life-affirmative in the midst of all the devious contradictions to which the modern society is heir to is a creditable achievement on the part of Williams. He has drawn a very interesting character-sketch of Amanda. She is witty, incisive in her comments; and at the same time, full of bubbling emotions for her daughter and son. On occasions, she had verbal skirmish either with her daughter or son; and being proud hereditarily, she stood firmly on her comments; but as soon as the daughter or the son came to her with due regrets for their behaviour, she got instantaneously melted. In scene four, one comes across such a situation with cathartic possibility.

After Tom had apologised to his mother : "I'm sorry for what I said, for everything that I said, I didn't mean it," Amanda spoke sobbingly : "My devotion has made me witch and so I make myself hateful to my children :

Tom : No, you *don't.*

Amanda : I worry so much, don't sleep, it makes me nervous.

Tom : (*gently*) I understand that.

Amanda : I've had to put up a solitary battle all these years. But you're my right hand bower. Don't fall down, don't fail.

Tom : (*gently*) I try, Mother.

Amanda : (*with great enthusiasm*) Try and you will succeed. (*The notion makes her breathless*) Why, you — you're just full of natural endowments. Both of my children — they're unusual children. Don't you think, I know it? I'm — proud. Happy and — feel I've — so much to be thankful for but — promise me one thing, son." And on being queried by Tom, "What, Mother ?", she said : "Promise, son, you'll — never be a drunkard" (1837).

The conversation between the mother and the son continued on a note of emotional intimacy. For a while, Tom agreed to say that he would not be a drunkard and that he would be satisfied by drinking coffee; and when he repeated : "Just coffee, Mother." On Amanda's suggestion that she should also take "shredded wheat biscuits" along with coffee; and finding that he was harping on drinking coffee alone, Amanda spoke in a practical sense : "You can't put in a day's work on an empty stomach. You've got ten minutes — don't gulp. Drinking too hot liquids makes cancer of the stomach. Put cream in" (1837). From Tom's health point of view, she was talking basic sense; but being mother, she was keenly solicitous that her son grows healthy, wealthy and wise. However, as her son Tom Wingfield was a poet while being engaged in a job at a warehouse, he used to go at times aberrant in his behaviour, he persisted in saying that he would prefer to take coffee only black; then, Amanda out of her motherly concern for him spoke : "I know, but it's (black coffee) not good for you. We have to do all that we can to build ourselves up. In these trying times we live in, all that we have to cling to is — each other.... That's why it's important to — Tom, I — I sent out your sister so I could discuss something with you..." (1857).

Even though the play, *The Glass Menagerie* ends on an uncertain note; still it has brighter spots too. Among the characters, the fully drawn one is that of Amanda. She was intelligent, affirmative and purposive. She very well understood the ways in which Tom and Laura were mentally working; and so, she tried her best to give them a sense of direction. To Tom, she confided about Laura : "You know how Laura is. So quiet but — still water runs deep. She notices things and I think she — broods about them. A few days ago I came in and she was crying.... She has an idea that you're not happy here." And on Tom's inquiring "What gave her that idea?" (1858)

Amanda then explained : "...you do act strangely, I — I'm not criticizing, understand that. I know your ambitions do not lie in the warehouse, that like everybody in the whole wide world — you've had to — make sacrifices, but — Tom — life's not easy, it calls for — Spartan endurance" (1858). It means rigorous regimen of life which Tom's father lacked, for he was given to wayward ways including drinking. It is in this context Amanda pleaded with Tom to note :

> "And you — when I see you taking after his ways. Staying out late — and — well, you had been drinking the night you were in that — terrifying condition. Laura says that you hate the apartment and that you go out nights to get away from it. Is that true Tom?" (1858)

On the basis of all these extracts, it is very clear that through the character of Amanda, the playwright has shown with skillful logic that one should have a positive and affirmative life-outlook; otherwise the alternative is disastrous indeed. All the characters — Amanda, Laura and Tom Wingfield are alienated; but as Amanda stuck fast to the practicable and positive side of life, she was able to provide a sense of direction to her children.

In the play, *A Streetcar Named Desire,* the elements of affirmation come out in a forceful manner through the different dramatic situations and through such a character, as DuBois Blanche. She became a victim of jealousy and hatred of her brother-in-law, Stanley Kowalski who ultimately disabled her through his beastly violence on her body. Being sophisticated and educated, she has a sneaking contempt for her sister, Stella's husband, Stanley. Because of her refined embellishments, Blanche landed herself into unseemly situations; and as a result, she suffered much and got alienated. Withal the play of negative elements she became prey to them, as a result of the Belle Reve estate's disintegration, she had certain parts in her that can be cited in defence of her possessing positive elements too. They mostly arise out of her intellectual refinement. In scene four of the play, *A Streetcar Named Desire,* one finds Blanche absorbingly engaged in conversation with her sister, Stella and the subject of their talk was Stanley Kowalski and his mode of crude behaviour. From the conversational extract being cited, it is possible to make an assessment of Blanche's viewpoint which is quite different to her sister, Stella's. It is revelatory of her refinement which in the scale of cultural evaluation stands on the affirmative side.

Blanche : Stella, I can't live with him! You can, he's your husband. But how could I stay here with him, after last night, with just those curtains between us?

Stella : Blanche, you saw him at his worst last night.

Blanche : On the contrary, I saw him at his best; what such a man has to offer is animal force and he gave a wonderful exhibition of that. But the only way to live with such a man is to — go to bed with him. And that's your job — not mine.

...I take it for granted that you still have sufficient memory of Belle Reve to find this place and these poker players impossible to live with (*BAP* 69).

It all shows that Blanche was in deadly contempt of Stanley just as he was having inveterate hatred of her; but in this tussle Stella was in conciliatory mood to both of them — one being sister and the other, her husband. She was certainly on the horns of a dilemma. Precisely, she told her sister : "But there are things that happen between a man and woman in the dark — that sort of make everything else seem — unimportant (Pause)" (70). It shows that she was trying to defend her role as a well-adjusted wife to Stanley; but at the same time, she was also attached to Blanche as sister. It is true that the two sisters differed greatly; still they had got affectionate feelings towards each other. After a pause, Blanche's comments get more cutting and scintillating on Stanley as also on man-woman relationship in general. Williams has made the dramatic situation arising out one's liking and disliking — as was the relationship between Blanche and Stanley Kowalski — theatrically more exciting in the sense that as Stella and Blanche were absorbingly busy in their conversation, Stanley overheard them remaining unseen. Her point of view may be a little bit extreme, still there is a merit in what she says. It affirms the tender side of femininity. To this extent, it is definitely affirmative :

Blanche : What you are talking about is brutal — just — Desire — the name of that rattle-trap streetcar that bangs through the quarter, up one old narrow street and down another....

Stella : Haven't you ever ridden on that streetcar?

Blanche : It brought me here. — Where I'm not wanted and where I'm ashamed to be....

Stella : Then don't you think your superior attitude is a bit out of place?

Blanche : I am not being or feeling at all superior, Stella. Believe me I'm not. It's just this. This is how I look at it. A man like that is someone to go out with — once, — twice — three times when the devil is in you. But live with ? Have a child by?

Stella : I have told you I love him.

Blanche : Then I tremble for you. I just — tremble for you (70).

It means there is a wide difference between the two sisters in regard to woman's attitude towards personal relationship with man. Even as Stella was not as much crude as her husband, Stanley was; nonetheless, she was not as much sophisticated as Blanche. It is because of this differing attitude, Stella — in self-justification spoke : 'I can't help your trembling if you insist on trembling.' Not pacified by Stella's comments; and getting a clearance from her sister, Blanche remarked : 'Well — if you' forgive me — he's common! Stella took it somewhat indifferently while her sister, already much disturbed, continued her diatribe against Stanley, providing due allowance for her sister's susceptibility as she spoke : '...You can't have forgotten that much of our bringing up, Stella, that you just *suppose* that any part of a gentleman's in his nature! *Not one particle,* no! Oh, if he was just — ordinary! Just plain — but good and wholesome but — no. There's something downright — bestial — about him! You're hating me saying this, aren't you?.... He acts like an animal; has an animal's habits! Eats like one, moves like one, talks like one!" (70)

From the conventional point of view, it all sounds as if she was hysterical and abnormal; but on a closer understanding of female psyche, it is possible to commisserate with her in her expression which moved avalanche-like from one stage to another. Not remaining satisfied in calling Stanley an animal with animal-like habits, she chose to assess him in terms of anthropological analysis : 'There's even something — sub-human — something not quite to the stage of humanity yet! Yes, something — ape-like about him, like one of those pictures I've seen in — anthropological studies ! Thousands and thousands of years have passed him right by, and there he is — Stanley Kowalski — survivor of the stone age. Bearing the raw meat home from the kill in the jungle. And you. You were waiting for him. May be he'll strike you or may be grunt and kiss you. That is, if kisses have been discovered yet. Night falls and the other apes gather. There in the front of the cave, all grunting like him, and swilling and gnawing and hulking. His poker night, — you call it — this party of apes. Somebody growls — some creature snatches at something — the fight is on. God! may be we are a long way from being made in God's image, but Stella — my sister — there has been *some* progress since then" (70).

In terms of sober assessment, it may sound a little bizarre for a sister-in-law to call her brother-in-law an ape with ape-like habits, whiling away his free-time in the company of poker players who were also made the butt of her ridicule — "all grunting like him, and swilling and gnawing and hulking...in front of the cave." She did not spare them also simply because as a highly sensitive, individualised woman she could not suffer the grouping of hefty characters with Stanley as their ring-leader. Out of fear of their physical force and unsophisticated temperament, Blanche felt a little agitated; and as she was sophisticated enough to think and feel, she found herself at a great distance from Stanley Kowalski and his play-mates. It is in this context her judgment on people like Stanley and his friends holds true : "Such things as art — as poetry and music — such kinds of new light have come into the world since then. In some kinds of people some tender feelings have had some little beginning. That we have got to make grow! and cling to and hold as our flag! In this dark march toward whatever it is we're approaching....*Don't — don't hang back with the brutes*!" (70)

In spite of all aberrations and abnormalities in *A Streetcar Named Desire,* one thing is maintainable that Blanche DuBois was a female character with distinctive and praiseworthy features to her credit. This holds true in spite of the maligning of her character by men like Stanley. To say that she was a washedout character would be improper. Even if she strayed away from the mores and manners of the social convention owing to precipitous changes in her life it would be immoral to blackmail her, as was the case with Stanley who tried to tarnish her image out of all proportion. One cannot say that she was sententious; but this much can be said in her defence that she was actually conscious of her environment at Stella's place. At the time when she was toying with the possibility of marriage with Mitch — which was sabotaged by Stanley — she told Stella on her marital interest in Mitch : "...Stella, I want his respect. And men don't want anything they get too easy. But on the other hand men lose interest quickly. Especially when the girl is over thirty. They think a girl over thirty ought to — the vulgar term is — 'put out.' ...and I — I'm not 'putting out' " (73).

The way Blanche DuBois puts in perspective her relationship with Mitch and the expectations she entertains in her mind shows that she had a practical sense; and that she did not want to be socially ostracised. On the common plane of thinking, she may be considered abnormal; but from the higher cultural point of view, she had the making of an uncommon character. Those who have read the novel, *Jude the Obscure,* by Thomas Hardy, would find a striking similarity of Blanche DuBois with Sue Bridehead in Hardy's novel. In this study of Thomas Hardy's novels, D.H. Lawrence has observed : "Sue had a being, special and beautiful.... Why was there no place for her? Cassandra had the Temple of Apollo. Why are we so foul that we have no reverence for that which we are and for that which is against us? If we had reverence for our life, our life would take at once religious form" (Phoenix 510).

Blanche DuBois in *A Streetcar Named Desire* tried to struggle herself to come to a religious view of life as a living individual and not merely a social fixture as the conventional viewpoint make a woman to be. Blanche DuBois did not want to be fixed as a social fixture. She was above the common rut of femininity. She paid the price for being uncommon; and *pro tanto,* she invited nemesis on herself. The adherents of the social convention like Stanley Kowalski living too much in the obvious do not approve of the finer shades of feelings and thoughts which Blanche embodied. As a result she was disabled by Stanley for life. Cultural nuances of finer feelings are as much necessary as the physical brute force. In the context of spirit and soul, human life needs the beneficent influences of refinement, poetry, music and art more compellingly than living a life of mere sensations and brute force. It is in this context Blanche DuBois is life-affirmatory and not freakish as her detractors tried hard to depict her.

After having studied Williams' plays : *The Glass Menagerie* and *A Streetcar Named Desire* in terms of alienation at different levels of human life; and then, alienation in the context of the spirit of affirmation in his characters as it comes out in his plays, it becomes possible to assess critically the phenomenon of alienation and its being overcome by the spirit of affirmation in the other major plays of Williams. In fact, Williams has tried out to project some of the basic issues of his personal life dressing it with poetic imagination. In his early life, he came face to face with the implications arising out of the parental conflict. As a consequence of it, Williams came to experience the complex skein of love, affection, hatred, personal likes and dislikes at the family level; and as he grew up, he became increasingly conscious of the wider social conflicts. In the white-hot furnace of his imagination, various conflicts and problems of his time got forged; and they got visualised aesthetically in a meaningful and satisfying manner. Because of his widely awakened conscience, he felt lonely to the bitterest degree; and as a result, he indulged in way-wardness also; but as he got a taste of literary creativity, he could transmute some of his deeply felt experience of alienation in his dramatic art. Through the medium, Williams has also conveyed snatches of heroic defiance in very difficult situations.

The criss-crossed conflicts arising out of the interplaying of social environment on human beings who differ from one another in several ways like differences of sex, race and creed provide dramatic background for Williams whereby he is able to create living characters. If one examines the motives and responses of Williams' characters, one finds in them the effect of alienation operating at different levels of sensibility; and as they wrestle with its impact, they react and respond differently because of the particular set of circumstances and situation in which they are placed. Williams was acutely conscious of this spectrum of life; and so he has been able to create characters of absorbing interest. In the course of affirming their destiny, they come into clash either with the hostile atmosphere or with characters pirated against them. In this way, they are able to show their mettle and grit of character. Thus, in Williams' plays one finds characters and situations so finely interfused with elements of alienation and acts of self-affirmation. By virtue of powerful imagination, Williams has been able to create characters life-like. For this reason, his plays have been widely acclaimed by all ranks of people. In his plays, the aspect of man's conflict with fate is brilliantly projected. He is a gifted playwright "...(who) is endlessly in pursuit of freedom — freedom from arbitrary values" (Lewis 13), be it of social convention or of science and technology as well as of state machinery. The psychological tussle between alienation and affirmation is essentially linked to different types of conflicts; and out of them, is forged man's determination to affirm his life in the midst of heavy odds. This is the message of Tennessee Williams in *The Glass Menagerie* and *A Streetcar Named Desire* and other writings.

## NOTE

1. The reference is to the period of depression in the thirties, when the huge middle class of America was matriculating in a school for the blind. Their

eyes had failed, or they had failed their eyes, and so they were having their fingers forcibly down on the fiery Braille alphabet of a dissolving economy.

## WORKS CITED

Lawrence, D.H., *Phoenix.* London : William Heinemann Ltd., 1968.

Lewis, Allan, Introduction, *American Plays and Playwrights of the Contemporary Theatre.* New York : Crown Publishers, Inc., 1970.

Williams, Tennessee. *The Glass Menagerie.* In *Concise Anthology of American Literature.* New York : Macmillan Pub. Co., 1985. Cited as *CAAL.*

——, *A Streetcar Named Desire* In *Best American Plays.* Third Series. Ed. John Gassner. New York : Crown Publications, Inc., 1963. Cited as *BAP.*

——, *Memoirs.* Garden City, New York : Doubleday, 1975.

# 3

# Arthur Miller's Handling of the Problem of Guilt

*—Gunjan Agarwal*

THE MAJOR part of the discussion relating to the 'disintegration and alienation at the family level' would mainly be confined to Miller's plays — *Death of a Salesman* (1949) and *All My Sons* (1947) even as contextual references may be necessary from other plays like — *The Crucible* (1953) and *A View From the Bridge* (1955). The play, *Death of a Salesman* is a classic example of the family situation in which disintegration and alienation among the main characters arise in tangible form. "The most important single fact about the plays of Arthur Miller is that he has brought back into the theatre, in an important way, the drama of social questions. It has been fashionable, certainly in England, to reject such drama as necessarily superficial. In part, this rejection is in itself social, for it has shown itself in the context of a particular phase of consciousness — that widespread withdrawal from social thinking, which came to its peak in the late nineteen-forties, at just the time when we were first getting to know Arthur Miller as a dramatist" (Williams 313).

In the context of social drama and tragedy, there had come to develop an erroneous viewpoint, that the high peak of tragic action just cannot be conveyed through a social play based on the life of common man. Miller has very trenchantly argued in the introduction to his *Collected Plays* (1956) that even Willy Loman, the hero of the play, *Death of a Salesman,* had the making of a tragic hero. This is what Miller says : "...this man is actually a very brave spirit who cannot settle for half, but must pursue his dream of himself to the end. Finally, ...this was no dumb brute heading mindlessly to his catastrophe" (*CP* 34).

However, in order to understand properly, the force and the pressure of 'disintegration and alienation in the play,' it would be better to bear in mind the main events attending to the development of the story in the play. "It opens with Willy Loman's return to his Brooklyn home after an abortive start on a selling trip. Willy is sixty-three, and just cannot summon the concentration and the will to go on selling, even to go on driving his car. Flashbacks give glimpses of happier days, when Willy's two boys (sons) were growing up, Biff, the high school football star, and Happy, the worshipful younger brother. Their mother, Linda, was also happy; the household was also thriving" (Shipley 420).

They were the good old days, when Willy Loman along with his wife and two sons was in his best of spirit. As if the gods sportingly desired that this successful salesman should also experience unsuccess in his wan days. His promising son, Biff, with his growing awareness as youthful son found fault with his aging father. "Then Biff, rushing to his father in a crisis, discovers him with another woman, calls him a 'phony', turns into a petty thief, and leaves home." Biff might have found himself as a farmer, but some family bond always brings him back, to quarrel with his father and leave again. Happy has grown into a self-centered lecher. Linda, loving and understanding, defends him against the contempt of his sons, but can bring nothing of sustain Willy, as he wonders vaguely and glumly about the downward turn of life. Finally, his salesmanship slumps so low that he cannot even persuade himself to go on living. His insurance, he comes to think, makes Willy "worth more dead than alive" (Shipley 420-21).

Miller has rendered the dramatic story of Willy Loman not in linear chronology but in terms of his inner experience; he lives through the past while wrestling with the present problems. In this way, he lives through the past, present and future. Being intensely aware of the baffling problems he was faced with, he heaved a sigh of relief in getting enkindled by the flashes of the past when the conditions were much better. As a result of this past-present-future continuum, he saved himself from much of the banality of personal and social life. However, it has also to be taken into account that as a result of living through the past with hopes of a better future, his sense of alienation got accentuated. The disillusionment with the boys, particularly with Biff put Willy into an unenviably bad equation of life. In fact, Biff's calling him 'phoney' had a dagger-like wound in his heart. When Miller in his introduction to Act I of this play says : "A word-sigh escapes his lips — it might be 'Oh, boy, oh, boy' " (*CP* 131), it apparently explains Willy Loman's pain, frustration and suffering. To say the least, Biff's highly uncharitable comment on his seeing father with another woman is in highly bad taste.

It dilapidated Willy very much, for he was very sensitive and given to certain ideals. He was devoted to his family; and if a son takes an impersonal and public view of his father's association with another woman, it shows he lacks faith in filial bonds. If Hamlet, in Shakespeare's play, arraigned his mother Gertrude for playing false to his father, there was moral justification for him to do so. But, in this play, Biff had no moral right to accuse his father for being with another woman because in the context of modern commercial milieu, more so in America, women move in and move out in diverse ways. Moreover, on the basis of Hamletian analogy, it can be safely stated that Willy Loman at no stage tried to threaten or harm his wife; rather he was very much devoted to her; for his wife, Linda was very much privy to him in all matters, nor did she suspect Willy's bonafides as husband. In the same way, Willy Loman was also committed totally to the well-being of the entire family.

When John Beaufort, the critic for the *Christian Science Moniter*, attacked "Willy Loman as a sad character, a vicious character...." Arthur Miller tried to disabuse of entertaining such a notion, by explaining : "The trouble with Willy Loman is that he has tremendously powerful ideals. We are not accustomed to speaking of ideals in his terms, but if Willy Loman, for instance, had not had a very profound sense that his life as lived had left him hollow, he would have died contentedly polishing his car on some Sunday afternoon at a ripe old age. The fact is that he has values. The fact that they cannot be realized is what is driving him mad, just as, unfortunately, it is driving a lot of other people mad. The truly valueless man, the man without ideals, is always perfectly at home anywhere because there cannot be conflict between nothing and something. Whatever negative qualities there are in the society or in the environment didn't bother him because they are not in conflict with any positive sense that he may have. I think Willy Loman is seeking for a kind of ecstasy in life which the machine civilization deprives people of" (Weales 175).

Miller has a smashing point that Willy Loman had the living fibers to be free of the inanemic desultoriness that human beings in general are prey to in the highly competitive machine civilisation of today. In spite of the offsetting situations he had to face, day to day, he did not shrink from his family responsibilities nor did he go gaga. He knew he had problems; but he did not escape from them. Even Biff's unceremonious comment, he tried to swallow; but, of course, with a deeply scarred fissure in his mind. It all shows that Willy had a livingly vibrant self. "He is looking for his selfhood, for his immortal soul, so to speak, and people who don't know the intensity of that quest think he is odd, but a lot of salesman, in a line of work where ingenuity and individualism are acquired by the nature of work, have a very intimate understanding of his problem; ...a salesman is a kind of creative person. ....they are; they have to get up in the morning and conceive a plan of attack and use all kinds of ingenuity all days long just like a writer does" (Weales 175-76).

From this extract, Miller has shown that Willy Loman was a creative salesman. He was not as cynical in his profession as the experts in standard American advertising want a salesman to be. Since, Willy had to maintain himself and his family as a salesman, he had to make good of the job. For him, salesmanship was just a technique to be mastered in order to survive as a family man. Had he adopted 'salesmanship' as a vicious strategy to outsell other products socially viable and of quality for the general good through doubtful techniques? "Technique is like anything else; it is deceitful only when it is used for deceitful purposes" (Weales 175).

To say the least, Willy Loman was not a deceitful person. From the study of Dickensian characters of doubtful worth, as it is very well found out from Dickens' novel like *The Old Curiosity Shop* (1841), *Martin Chuzzlewit* (1844), *Bleak House* (1853), *Hard Times* (1854) and *Our Mutual Friend* (1865), it is ascertainable that a man of family interested in the well-being of his dependents would not indulge in deceitful selling. It is in terms of this assessment that Miller points out : "Willy is a baby, I mean, Willy is naive enough to believe in the goodness of his mission. There are highly paid advertising people who are utterly cynical about the business, and probably a lot of people call Willy vicious who would think of themselves as simply the plans of society. Willy is a victim; he didn't originate this thing. He believes that selling is the greatest thing anybody can do" (Weales 176).

It is a revealing comment by the dramatist on his favourite character. The important point is that Willy Loman is naive. Just because he is naive, it is possible to conjecture on the basis of human experience that he must have been disliked by such of his friends who have whittled down their innate sense of naivete, who prefer to play clever with others, as is generally the case with a lot of people in today's world. One thing striking with clever people is that as they remain immune to the pangs of conscience, they can attune themselves to any situation including insulting behaviour. In this way, they remain unamenable to any kind of alienated experience.

This was not so with Willy Loman, for he was a man of conscience and self-respect. He suffered the pangs of loneliness and alienation at different levels of experience. At a number of places in the body of the play, Willy Loman is seen undergoing the alienated feeling. Already a reference has been made to

Willy's heaving a sigh of sadness with words, 'Oh, boy, oh, boy', at the beginning of this chapter. In the same way, Willy after his abortive selling trip, he is seen talking with his wife; then, elated with wonder speaks almost spasmodically : "I was driving along, you understand? And I was fine. I was even observing the scenery. You can imagine, me looking at scenery, on the road every week of my life. But it is so beautiful up there, Linda, the trees are so thick, and the sun is warm. I opened the windshield and just let the warm air bathe over me. And then all of a sudden I'm goin' off the road! I'm tellin' ya, I absolutely forgot I was driving. If I'd've gone the other way over the white line I might've killed somebody. So I went on again — and five minutes later I'm dreamin' again, and I nearly — He presses two fingers against his eyes. I have such thoughts, I have such strange thoughts" (*CP* 132).

The way Willy Loman expresses his feelings in zigzag and crisscross manner is indicative of his highly-strung perturbed state of mind. The fine verbal expressionism conveyed through 'I have such thoughts, I have such strange thoughts' imparts a highly dignified and kingly stature to this salesman. It also shows his deeper involvement in the life processes of his past and the present with an eye on future. In a highly competitive society, a salesman conscious of his family responsibility finds himself at cross-purposes with the contingent pressures operating from outside over which an individual has hardly any control.

Since he was hard pressed by the compulsive need to earn more money to meet the increasing liability arising out of recurring and fixed expenditure; and since he found himself unable to cope with the increasing demand for money, owing to the sea-change having crept in at the management level following the passing away of the old Wagner and the entrenchment of his son Howard who chose to remain impersonal to the working conditions and operational problems of Willy Loman.

Even at home, he found himself distracted; partly it was the overwhelming impact of money shortage. He had laid much hope on his elder son, Biff to be self-sufficient in earning; but on this issue, he found himself at odds with him. When his wife, Linda in a sympathetic appraisal of the difficulties and tensions in their family life said : 'Well, dear, life is a casting off. It's always been that way', the trend of their conversation took a homeward turn :

Willy : No, no, some people — some people accomplish something. Did Biff say anything after I went this morning?

Linda : You shouldn't have criticized him Willy especially after he just got off the train. You mustn't lose temper with him.

Willy : When the hell did I lose my temper? I simply asked him if he was making any money. Is that criticism? (*CP* 133)

His wife tried to assuage his feelings about Biff not coming to his expectations; still Willy was unable to find himself with Biff's way of prospecting himself. Significantly enough, Willy observed : "How can he find himself on a farm? Is that a life? A farmhand? In the beginning, when he was young, I thought, well, a young man, it's good for him to tramp around, take a lot of different jobs. But it's more than ten years now and he has yet to make thirty-five dollars a week" (*CP* 134).

His wife again and again tried to soft-pedal Willy's feelings towards Biff; but her husband, being still unreconciled with Biff chose to observe on him critically and reminiscently : "Biff Loman is lost. In the greatest country in the world a young man with such — personal attractiveness, gets lost. And such a hard worker. There's one thing about Biff — he's not lazy."

Linda : Never.

Willy : (*with pitty and resolve*). I'll see him in the morning; I'll have a nice talk with him. I'll get him a job selling. He could be big in no time. My God! Remember how they used to follow him around in high school? When he smiled at one of them their faces lit up. When he walked down the street.... (*He loses himself in remembrances*... (*CP* 134).

This is a highly relevant extract for understanding the intensely alienated personality of Willy Loman. The experiential content in such a person would be really lacerating for him to bear with. One can understand the plight of Willy Loman from a parallel example of a person who had earlier seen the good days of life and when by an ill-fate he enters the rut of poverty. For such a man, this type of adverse change means the ballistic fall of a catastrophe.

Willy Loman as father was good at heart. At no stage, he wanted to hamper the progress of his two sons. All he could do in the hour of his decline was to encourage them to be good and to be prosperous. But, Biff, with lesser severity, and also Happy, failed to understand the sentiments of their father. It is true that in the actual conditions of the present-day secularised industrial society, the younger generation fails to respect those who are elderly.[1]

Through the medium of Willy, it appears, Arthur Miller has also highlighted the ravages of urban civilisation. A man of fairly good sensibility as Willy was, is liable to get disenchanted with the surroundings :

> Willy : The street is lined with cars. There's not a breath of fresh air in the neighbourhood. The grass don't grow any more, you can't raise a carrot in the backyard. They should've had a law against apartment houses. Remember these two beautiful elm trees out there? When I and Biff hung the swing between them?
>
> Linda : Yeah, like being a million miles from the city.
>
> Willy : They should've arrested the builder for cutting those down. They massacred the neighbourhood. (Lost) : More and more I think of those days, Linda. This time of year it was lilac and wisteria. And then the peonies would come out, and the daffodils. What fragrance in this room! (*CP* 134-35)

It was in the days gone by the surroundings were good, and so citizens were homely, joyous and less fractious than now. This is how Willy felt. He considered the growth in population one of the factors responsible for lack of nature's healing bounty, though his wife felt otherwise. "I don't think there's more people," as Linda contended. But, Willy had his own say : "There's more people! That's what ruining this country! Population is getting out of control. The competition's maddening! Smell the stink from the apartment house! And another one on the other side.... How can they whip cheese?" (*CP* 135)

Willy is discomfited by the impact of population and denudation of nature in urban centres. In this respect, his wife Linda is not much concerned with. Apparently, this difference in attitude to the surroundings is because the psyche of man and that of woman are different to this aspect of life. Furthermore, Willy being a salesman, had to hop at pressure point from one place to another; and for this reason, he was more interested in maintaining a living rapport with plants and trees. In this way, the content of privacy comes more insistently on male psyche than on that of female.

The more the man is disturbed and distracted, the more he needs the healing fragrance of privacy. This observation, of course, needs to be qualified by the fact of a particular man to be free from the shares of debauchery. The way Willy Loman meanders in his conversation with his wife is indicative of his not being a debauch. His wife did not doubt his integrity; even though one of his sons, for example Biff may have his own reasons to suspect him of this nasty viciousness, his other son Happy did not take it that way.

Miller has very ingenuously webbed the warp and woof of the dramatic story in a way to show the extremely distracted mental condition of Willy. In the course of conversing with his wife, while remaining meaningfully rational, he suddenly gets into apostrophising in the past, as it is shown here :

Linda : And Willy — if it's warm Sunday we'll drive in the country. And we'll open the windshield, and take lunch.

Willy : No, the windshields don't open on the new cars.

Linda : But you opened it today.

Willy : Me? I didn't. (*He stops*). Now isn't that peculiar! Isn't that remarkable — (He breaks off in amazement and fright as the flute is heard distantly).

Linda : What, darling?

Willy : That is the most remarkable thing.

Linda : What, dear?

Willy : I was thinking of the Chevvy. (*Slight pause*). Nineteen twenty-eight...when I had that red Chevvy-(*Breaks off*). That funny? I could sworn I was driving that Chevvy today.

Linda : Well, that's nothing. Something must've reminded you.

Willy : Remarkable. Remember those days? The way used to simonize that car? The dealer refused to believe there was eighty thousand miles on it. (*He shakes his head*). Heh! (*To Linda*) : Close your eyes, I'll be right up. (*He walks out of the bedroom*) (*CP* 135-36).

Willy is unto himself, lonely and lost in himself completely. It all shows that the man divorces himself for a while from his present distractions and enters the happy days he had in the past. Off and on, Willy re-lives his past to prepare himself for a better future. When one's past is happier than the present, one is saved; one is saved from getting lurched into cynicism. The dramatist in terms of his dramatic technique has very sensitively delineated the behaviour and movement of Willy Loman.

In terms of the preceding sequence, Willy Loman found himself alone after he had left his wife in the bedroom. The dramatic scene is altered to impart the dramatic impact : "*Light has risen on the boys room. Unseen, Willy is heard talking to himself, 'Eighty thousand miles,' and a little laugh. Biff gets out of bed, comes downstage a bit, and stands attentively*" (*CP* 136). Feeling estranged from his father, Biff tries to decipher the meaning of his father's soliloquous utterance : " 'Eighty thousand miles.' A little later, in the living-room : Yes, sir, eighty thousand miles — eighty-two thousand" (*CP* 137).

While Willy was uttering these words, he got the impression that his two sons were in conversation :

Happy : (*getting out of bed*) He's going to get his license taken away if he keeps that up. I'm getting nervous about him, y'know, Biff?

Biff : His eyes are going.

Happy : No, I've driven with him. He sees all right. He just doesn't keep his mind on it. I drove into the city with him last week. He stops at a green light and then it turns red and he goes. (*He laughs*).

Biff : May be he's color-blind.

Happy : Pop? Why? He's got the finest eye for color in the business. You know that.

.... .... .... ....

Biff : Why does Dad mock me all the time?

Happy : He's not mocking you, he —

Biff : Everything I say there is a twist of mockery on his face. I can't get near him.

Happy : He just wants you to make good, that's all. I wanted to talk to you about Dad for a long time, Biff. Something's — happening to him. He — talks to himself.

Biff : I noticed that this morning. But he always mumbled (*CP* 137-38).

.... .... .... ....

From the tenor of conversation between Biff and Happy, it is found that Biff was somewhat more disenchanted with his father than it was so with Happy. All the same, Happy tried to convince his elder brother that their father was more concerned about Biff. What Willy wanted was that his elder son, Biff should get settled in an earning capacity, for he was already thirty-four. Biff had a feeling that his father may be partly justified; for Willy was a success-dreamer like many of his compatriots. With this American attitude in him, it was possible for Willy as father to have been sorely disappointed with Biff for his lack of initiative in earning his own living.

Miller has used this estrangement between Biff and his father Willy, the highly disintegrating and pressurising aspects of the American economy on family life. Since a large number of people in America have to eke out their existence with very little money to fall back upon, they get fixated about their future in the turmoil of socio-economic forces unleashed by the increasing inflation and hectic competition. If Willy had his own compelling necessity to expect Biff to be more actively concerned with his earning. Biff had his own justification in failing to get up.

In his own defence, Biff tries to explain his position :

> Biff : Well, I spent six or seven years after high school trying to work myself up. Shipping, clerk, salesman, business of one kind or another. And it's a measly manner of existence. To get on that subway on the hot mornings in summer. To devote your whole life to keeping stock, or making phone calls, or selling or buying. To suffer fifty weeks of the year for the sake of a two-week vacation, when all you really desire is to be outdoors, with your shirt off. And always to have to get ahead of the next fella. And still — that's how you build a future (*CP* 138).

When Happy asked him how he had enjoyed his life on a farm, Biff narrated his farming experience in Nebraska, the Dakotas, Arizona and in Texas. While enjoying the most at the Texas farm, during the spring season, he also got a lurking feeling that he was not getting anywhere, "What the hell am I doing, playing around with horses, twenty-eight dollars a week! I'm thirty-four years old. I ought be makin' my future. That's when I come running home. And now, I got here and I don't know what to do with myself. (*After a pause*). I've always made a point of not wasting my life, and everytime I come back here I know that all I've done is to waste my life" (*CP* 139).

Biff is also lost, with the only difference, his father is finding himself at the fag-end of his life. That a young man, around thirty-four years should feel frustrated and wasted in a country, supposed to be the most powerful economy in the world of twentieth century, bespeaks of the social malaise that corrodes the fibers of social and family life.

The other son of Willy Loman is Happy. The first question that looms large about him is that — Is he really happy? He is not. In assessing Happy's standing as young man, two years junior to Biff, Arthur Miller observes : "Happy is tall, powerfully made. Sexuality is like a visible colour on him, or a scent that many women have discovered. He, like his brother, is lost, but in a different way, for he has never allowed himself to turn his face towards defeat and is thus more confused and hard-skinned, although seemingly more content" (*CP* 136).

Happy Loman desires an easy passage to prosperity. Responding to Biff's queries — "Are you content, Hap? You're a success, aren't you?" (*Happy moving about with energy, expressiveness*), said, : "All I can do now is wait for the merchandise manager to die. And Suppose, I get to be merchandise manager? He's a good friend of mine, and he just built a terrific estate on long Island. And he lived there about two months and sold it, and now he's building another one. He can't enjoy it once it's finished. And I know that's just what I would do. I don't know what the hell I'm workin' for. Sometimes I sit in my apartment — all alone. And I think of the rent I'm paying. And it's crazy. But then, it's what I always wanted. My own apartment, a car, and plenty of women. And still, goddammit, I'm lonely" (*CP* 139).

It all shows that Happy is equally lost and lonely. It all shows that Happy like Biff found himself in disarray out of tune with the actual environment. 'Money-commodity-money' momentus, as Marx came to recognise the sinewy power of modern capitalism, leads to the dehumanisation of life. Marx writes in *Capital*, "(Capitalism) squanders human lives, or living labour, and not only flesh and blood, but also nerve and brain.

Indeed it leads to the most enormous waste of the individual development" (Cohen 25). The subtle effects of the capitalistic system on man as individual is really frightening. Even as Marx saw in Capitalistic mode of production catalytic for taking the narrow feudal society forward, he also saw in its working "a long unspeakable human tragedy, in which the great majority of men and women are condemned to a life of wretched, fruitless toil. The division of labour maims and nourishes simultaneously, generating fresh skills and capacities but in a cripplingly one-sided way. The creative powers which enable humanity to control its environment, eradicating disease, famine, natural catastrophe, also enable it to prey upon itself. Each new medium of communication is at the same time an instrument of division and alienation" (Eagleton 219).

This assessment of the capitalistic impact on individual man and woman is frighteningly true, provided a reader is honest enough to evaluate the socio-economic environment on the plane of sensibility. It is in this background if one examines the reactions and responses of Biff and Happy to their family environment as well as to the larger profile of American economy in which there is a great scope for money-making. But at what cost? Willy was on his way to lose his poise and equilibrium. Biff and Happy were equally frustrated. While Biff was getting sententious and fault-finding, Happy was unhappy in his own way. Despite his being mentally whelmed with womanly presence, he found himself equally lonely and lost. Happy is not realistic; he misconstrues the talents and earning potential of an estate builder, supposed to be earning "fifty-two thousand dollars a year coming through the revolving door," and then, he boasts of his talents too : "and I got more in my pinky finger than he's got in his head" (*CP* 140).

In this way, one can say that in capitalistic system of society, young persons get easily money-struck; and through it, they get moon-struck — to put it metaphorically[2], and finally self-struck. Apparently, it results because of the failure in money-earning, frustration in love; and then, it paves the way for life in shambles. This is the result of indulging in self-deception. Happy is at least more candid about self-deception. "Manufacturers offer me a hundred-dollar bill now and then to throw an order their way. You know how honest I am, but it's like this girl, see. I hate myself for it. Because I don't want the girl, and still, I take it and — I love it" (*CP* 141).

In Happy's case as also in respect of other young Americans, their life goes shifty unless there is creative involvement in making a choice and then, remaining stuck to it, though initially, one may be daunted to face life squarely. It is typically a middle-class petti-bourgeois attitude. Money has its own importance but when money is made God, everything gets topsy-turvy and human values go in disarray. As a result of this attitude, family life gets fissured. In the dramatic story of *Death of a Salesman,* one finds through the observations of wife Linda made in her talking with her sons. Biff and Happy that their father, Willy was disintegrating under the pressure of adverse conditions of work — unsalaried, only getting commission at pitifully low rate.

She disabused Biff of his wrong notion that his father, Willy was now getting crazy. The only agonised aspect of his life was that being past sixty years, he was not able to attune himself to the compulsions of the commercial world as also to the increasing expectations of his two sons in disaffection with themselves. As to Biff's complaint that his father Willy was not kindly disposed towards him, Linda tried to assuage the estranged feelings of Biff : "When you write you're coming, he's all smiles, and talks about the future, and — he's just wonderful. And then the closer you seem to come, the more shaky he gets, and then, by the time you get here, he's arguing, and he seems angry at you. I think it's just may be he can't bring himself to — to open up to you. Why are you so hateful to each other? Why is that?" (*CP* 161)

Even as Biff tried to reassure his mother Linda that he was trying to change himself, she told him categorically that she loved Willy intensely : "He's the dearest man in the world to me, and I won't have anyone making him feel unwanted and low and blue. You've got to make up your mind now, darling, there's no leeway any more. Either he's your father, and you pay him that respect, or else you are not to come here. I know he's not easy to get along with — nobody knows that better than me" (*CP* 162).

Even Happy took cudgels on behalf of his father telling Biff that he needn't call him crazy. But, persisted in saying adversely against his father : "He's got no character — Charley wouldn't do this. Not in his own house — spewing out that vomit from his mind" (*CP* 162). Seeing that Biff was still unrepentant, Linda got chagrined to remark : "...I don't say he's a great man. Willy Loman never made a lot of money. His name was never in the paper. He's not the finest character that ever lived. But he's a human being, and a terrible thing is happening to him. So attention must be paid. He's not to be allowed to fall into his grave like an old dog. Attention, attention must be finally paid to such a person. You called him crazy —" (*CP* 162).

Linda took an opportunity of reminding her sons, specially Biff, to understand his father's actual condition. She put it realistically with a pinch of saltish pathos : "A small man can be just as exhausted as a great man. He works for a company thirty-six years this March, opens up unheard-of territories to their trademark, and now in his old age they take his salary away" (*CP* 163).

Biff and Happy were consternated to know that their father after having worked for the company for over thirty-six years was being deprived of the salary benefit in his old age, working only on the commission basis. Still, he maintained household facilities, like the appliance for hot-water system. Willy-Loman in his good-sense, did not allow his sons to feel the pinch of impecuniosity. If Willy bore all the suffering of earning money as salesman — getting physically weak — was it not being done for the sake of maintaining the family show without any unwarranted pestering of unscrupulous money-lenders which he didn't do in terms of commonsense? If in doing so, he got tensed and sometimes erratic in his behaviour, it was too much for his sons to laugh at him and for Biff to call him crazy.

Linda's oral apology tendered to her sons is revealing enough of the plight of Willy. He was getting exhausted by the overwhelming impact of adverse circumstances. If his sons were irresponsive to their father, the people in business were no less uncharitable towards this aging salesman, whose youthful fervour was no more in the midst of circumstances getting more and more complicated :

Linda : Are they any worse than his sons? When he brought them business, when he was young, they were glad to see him. But now his old friends, the old buyers that loved him so and always found some order to hand him in a pinch — they're all dead, retired. He used to be able to make six, seven calls a day in Boston. Now he takes his valises out of the car and puts them back and takes them out again and he's exhausted. Instead of walking he talks now. He drives seven hundred miles, and when he gets there, no one knows him any more, no one welcomes him. And what goes through a man's mind, driving seven hundred miles home without having earned a cent? Why shouldn't he talk to himself? Why? When he has to go to Charley and borrow fifty dollars a week and pretend to me that it's his pay? How long can that go on? How long? You see what I'm sitting here and waiting for? And you tell me he has no character? The man who never worked a day but for your benefit? When does he get the medal for that? Is this his reward — to turn around at the age of sixty-three and find his sons, who he loved better than his life, one a philandering bum :

Happy : Mom!

Linda : That's all you are, my baby (*CP* 163).

She further reminded Biff to know how he used to feel lonely until he could come home to you. This was in the past but now, was it justified that his son should suffer his very presence. As the play works it out, one finds that Miller is highly critical of the values of American society. Apparently, owing to their being too much engrossed with the seemy side of social life sustained on the glamorous pull of money and woman, it was no wonder that Willy should say to Linda : "You don't know the average caliber any more. The average young man today — he is getting into bed — is got a caliber of zero. Greatest thing in the world was to bum around" (*CP* 208). It is partly owing to the lack of purpose, and complacency on the part of middle class young men. Because of lack of personal involvement in the complicated processes of earning one's bread, they not only overestimate their talents but also take an easy view of the American world of commerce and industry.

On the whole, the play *Death of a Salesman* is a searing indictment of the modern American way of life. The damnable aspect of the American social conditions is that the family life has got coarsened because of the inroads of money-power and the values it brings in its fold. The delicate side of the inter-relationships between men and women, as well as between boys and girls has got dehydrated and commodified. In the name of love and affection, the youngsters try to show themselves 'sentimentalised' with tears lurking in their eye-lashes. And they call this emotive purgation. Is this not a maligned form of misunderstanding?

It is in this setting Willy Loman-Biff equation gets focused dramatically. Biff had come to his father to intercede on his behalf with Birnhaum so that he may not fail in maths. Quite strangely, at this material time, Biff found his father in tense conversation with a woman. This woman's remark to Biff : "Are you baseball or football?" was uncharitable to Willy's son. Then, she left the premises in a huff. After a pause, Willy without feeling unhinged tried to clear any misconception in the mind of son, Biff about the presence of a woman in Willy's premises. Biff was overworked with dismay and tears at this spectacle :

"Willy : (*After a pause*) Well, better get going. I want to get to the school first thing in the morning. Get my suits out of the closet. I'll get my valise. (*Biff doesn't move*). What's the matter? (*Biff remains motionless, tears falling*). She's a buyer. Buys for J.H. Simmons. She lives down the hall — they're painting. You don't imagine — (*He breaks off. After a pause*). Now listen, pal, she's just a buyer. She sees merchandise in her room and they have to keep it looking just so..... (*Pause Assuming command*). All right, get my suits. (*Biff doesn't move.*) Now stop crying and do as I say. I gave you an order. Biff, I gave you an order..... How dare you cry! (*Putting his arm around Biff*)..." (*CP* 208).

In this way, Willy as father to a grown-up son tried to pacify the distracted mind of Biff at the woman's episode by telling him that he should not 'overemphasise a thing like this' simply because there are certain 'shady' aspects of modern commercial life which would be clear to him with the passage of time when he would gain in maturity. Willy also tried to assure his son that he would do his best to get him success in the examination.

Willy, as father and salesman knew the complex character of modern commercial life. He tried to explain to his enraged son, the compulsions of events under which Biff found him with the woman. Biff's getting touchy over this episode was essentially a sign of his youthful immaturity. Had he been carrying within himself a sense of maturity, he would have tried to rationalize the unexpected situation — even worse than what actually occurred — in the way somewhat to that of the poetic wisdom of T.S. Eliot :

> ...Think now
> History has many cunning passages,
> contrived corridors
> And issues, deceives with whispering ambitions,
> Guides by vanities (Eliot 38).

After all, it was under the influence of vanity, Biff persisted in making a mountain out of a molehill. In terms of the dramatic scene, Biff should have been tolerant of the unwholesome situation arising out of his father's being in tense conversation with another woman at night. While Willy continued to soften the impact of woman's presence in his premises on Biff's mind by repeating that he would spare no efforts in getting him make up his study performance in summer school, Biff stuck to his sentimental resolve to see that his father is made to feel lowered in his eye. In a way, Biff wanted to put his father in the dock for very unascertainable reasons. The scene that follows this overworked response of Biff is still more damaging to the nearly lost equilibrium of Willy. Apparently, things were moving in such a direction. Willy's soothingly telling his son not to worry too much on his lack of performance in studies triggered his catharsis into his sadness :

Biff : (*his weeping breaking from him*) Dad....
Willy : (*infected by it*) Oh, my boy....
Biff : Dad....
Willy : She's nothing to me, Biff. I was lonely, I was terribly lonely.
Biff : You — you gave her Mama, stockings. (*His tears break through and he rises to go*)
Willy : (*grabbling for Biff*) I gave you an order!
Biff : Don't touch me, you — liar!
Willy : Apologize for that!
Biff : You fake! You phony little fake! (*Overcome, he turns quickly and weepingfully goes out with his suitcase. Willy is left on the floor on his knees*).
Willy : I gave you an order! Come back here or I'll beat you! Come back here! I'll whip you! (*CP* 208).

From this conversational extract and from the unsavoury news, Willy got from Stanley : "Your boys left with the chippies, they said they will see you home," he was saddened to remark : "But we were supposed to have dinner together" (*CP* 209). Relevantly enough, Happy's attitude towards his father is equally bad as that of his elder brother. In the course of an animated conversation, Biff and Happy were having with two girls — Letta and Miss Forsythe in the context of their father's growing alienation with them, the undernoted conversational piece between Letta and Happy is of more than usual significance :

Letta : Don't you want to tell your father —
Happy : No, that's not my father. He's just a guy. Come on, we'll catch Biff and Honey, we're going to paint this town! (*CP* 205)

On the strength of this piece, it is not far to find that both Biff and Happy were insulting their father. In their own ways, their attitude towards their struggling father smacked their filial disobedience. If Biff could show himself so much touchy about his seeing father in the company of another woman, it does also show that he himself sinned more disagreeably than Willy, for Biff called him, "You fake! You phony fake" (*CP* 208).

Since both Biff and Happy were demeaning in their behaviour towards their father in the grip of the last spasm of his life, one can say they were equally culpable, along with the highups in Willy's commercial world for his premature death. Their father passed away almost as a dog except for the kind-hearted and savoury behaviour of his wife Linda. In *Death of a Salesman,* there is full blast of alienation and family disintegration; whereas in *All My Sons,* this impact works on a slightly differing keel. The behaviour of Chris Keller and Larry remains swaddled with a stamp of romanticised idealism towards their father Joe Keller, for his lack of social responsibility in supplying defective airplane spares during the height of the second war. Otherwise, as far as the death aspect is concerned, the two tragic heroes — Joe Keller and Willy Loman laid down their lives for the sake of their families in the midst of alienation, innuendoes and unwarranted harshness.

## NOTES

1. In contemporary India one can also find scars of alienation among the elderly generation writ large on their faces. Some of them suffer King Lear-like!
2. Moonstruck means feminine obsession which deflects one from real purposes of life.

## WORKS CITED


Cohen, G.A., *Karl Marx's Theory of History : A Defence.* Oxford, 1978.

Eagleton, Terry, *The Ideology of the Aesthetic.* Oxford : Basil Blackwell Ltd., 1990.

Eliot, T.S., *Collected Poems* (1909-1935). London : Faber and Faber, 1958.

Miller, Arthur, *Collected Plays.* Cited as *CP.*

Shipley, Joseph T. ed., *The Crown Guide to the World's Great Plays.* New York : Crown Publishers, 1984.

Wiliams, Raymond, "The realism of Arthur Miller." *Text and Criticism on Arthur Miller's Death of a Salesman.* Ed. Gerard Weales. New York : Penguin Books, USA Inc., 1977. Cited as Weales.

# 4

# *The Bell Jar* and "Tongues of Stone" : A Comparative Study

*—N.B. Masal*

SYLVIA PLATH is a major American woman poet associated with the tradition of confessional poetry. Besides being a poet, she was also a fiction writer and story writer. She has wrote only novel *The Bell Jar* which is an autobiographical novel and also a collection of short stories. We see that a great deal of critical work has already been done on Sylvia Plath's Poetry. But comparatively, her novel and short stories have not received the kind of critical attention they deserve.

The present paper seeks to provide in what way there is a comparison between Sylvia Plath's novel *The Bell Jar* and her short story "Tongues of Stone," as included in her works *Johnny Panic and the Bible of Dreams.*

Ted Hughes indicates that Sylvia Plath, launched herself into *The Bell Jar* in 1960. But at least the four stories written between 1954 and 1959 deal with some of the same material. One in particular "Tongues of Stone" (1955), uses the experience of a young girl's nervous breakdown much as Plath uses it in *The Bell Jar.* In this story at least six key incidents appear first in this story, before being transformed and interpolated into the novel. The start of the breakdown is the same in both pieces. The main character is suffering from extreme apathy, anxiety. In *The Bell Jar* Esther enters the first Clinic, Walton, after three weeks of not sleeping. In "Tongues of Stone" the character is at end of two months of sleeplessness. In setting the scene of the "Tongues of Stone" the narrator explains :

> "It was sometime in October, she had long ago lost track of all the days and it really did not matter because one was like another and there were no nights to separate them because she never slept anymore" (*JPBD* 268).
>
> Both young women try to forestall their depression by looking for intellectual occupations to, literally, kill time. Each tries particularly hard to read, only to find the print on the pages of their books indecipherable, 'dead black hieroglysphs, and "fantastic untranslatable shapes, like Arabic and Chinese" (*BJ* 102).

Both are denied solace by their alienation from the dead intellectual world represented by the printed books. But more obvious in their similarities than these parallels of general circumstances are the active steps in their attempted suicides and their subsequent treatments. Looking at these steps, the reader can see Plath's movement from a rather flat narrative to the evocative and powerful voice of the novel. The apprentice piece has all the isolated units but does not have the developed style, theme or political focus of *The Bell Jar.*

First, in both "Tongues of Stone" and *The Bell Jar,* each of the girls visits her sleeping mother and comes to an important realization, there is neither parental security nor any meaningful reason to continue being in either the present or the future. In "Tongues of Stone", the main character sleeps into her mother's bed and, lying beside her, "Listening to the thin thread of her mother's breathing, wanting to get up and twist the life out of the fragile throat, to end at once the process of slow disintegration which grinned at her like a death's head everywhere she turned" (*JPBD* 271).

The girl (who remains nameless throughout the story), has sought out her mother. By getting close to her, the girl hopes to get over the fears and despair she feels. But the mother can neither solace nor protect her daughter. Asleep, she is even unaware of the girl's presence. She is perceived by her daughter as fragile and disintegrating, not a possible haven or shelter against the death of her daughter sees everywhere, even in her. This same incident occurs in *The Bell Jar,* but some of the narrator's feelings have changed. In the novel, the mother is less mutual victim, another fragile throat which can be stopped, and more a despised perpetrator of circumstances, a guardian of the world's values and actions. The main character, Esther looks at her sleeping mother, listens to her piggish snozes, and explains :

> ...for a while it seemed to me that the only way to stop it, the sound in her mother's throat would be to take the column of skin and sinew from which it rose and twist it to silence between my hands (*BJ* 101).

Not only is the mother more unattractive in this version being piggish and irritating, but the action of strangling her is not done to stop a mutual disintegration, a slow and painful change, but more to assuage Esther's aggressive dislike of what her mother represents. She and her mother are struggling against one another, tussling between then expectations for Esther's future and Esther's own desires. Neither is totally passive. Esther views the strangling not as euthanasia, but as means of effectively changing her own world. Where in "Tongues of Stone" the girl creeps into her mother's bed for solace, in *The Bell Jar,* Esther Greenwood merely looks at her mother from the bed-room door, not seeking communion with a source of safety so much as observing the enemy.

After this scene, both stories show the female protagonist trying to escape the world around her by hiding under the mattress of her bed. In each case, she hopes to be crushed, to never reawaken to the oppressive world of sleepless, meaningless, comfortless living. In "Tongues of Stone" the girl leaves her mother's bed, "Creeping back to her own bed, then, she had lifted up mattress, wedding herself in the crevices between mattress and bed springs, longing to be crushed beneath the heavy slab" (*JPBD* 271-72). More immediately the same scene is enacted in *The Bell Jar.*

> "I crawled between the mattress and in padded bedstead and let the mattress fall across me like a tombstone. It felt dark and safe under there, but the mattress was not heavy enough. It needed about a ton more weight to make me sleep" (*BJ* 101).

In the second scene, the tone is sharper. The slab has been defined as a tombstone, the oppression and death imagery are more overt. Plath's character recognizes consciously that what she is seeking is the safe dark of death and that it would take to achieve it about a ton more.

Both girls attempt suicide actually, reach out to take hold of the darkness, but are discovered at the last moment and saved. Upon first awakening from their drugged state, each believes herself blind. In "Tongues of Stone" the narrator explains that :

> "At first they thought she would be blind in that eye. She had lain awake the night of her second birth into the world of flesh, talking to a nurse who was sitting up with her, turning her sightless face toward the gentle voice and saying over and over again, "But I cannot see, I cannot see."

The nurse, who had also believed that she was blind, tried to comfort her, saying

> "There are a lot of other blind people in the world. You will meet a nice blindman and marry him some day" (*JPBD* 272).

In this scene the nurse is an acknowledged presence, someone known and staying with the girl, not just beside her. She is described as gentle and comforting, albeit not well-informed. This same scene is recreated in *The Bell Jar,* only this time the nurse's presence is not so immediately felt as sympathetic.

> "I opened my eyes.
> It was completely dark.
> Somebody was breathing beside me.
> I cannot see! I said —
> A cheery voice spoke out of the dark. There are lots of blind people in the world. You will marry a nice blind man some day" (*DJ* 140).

Although, the changes are slight, they do match up with the more sinister and detached feelings of Esther in the novel. The nurse in the second presentation is not known immediately, she is somebody. She is not with the girl she is beside her. Although she is cheery, unlike the original image of comforting presence, we have no reason to assume her intentions are personal; rather, they smack of habitual, professional cheeriness.

Each girl also tries to strangle herself, although the timing of the attempt varies. In "Tongues of Stone", the girl is in the sanatorium, frustrated and depressed that the insulin treatment is not working. She considers strangulation as a means to end the continuing depression and self-disgust :

> "One night she hid the pink cotton scarf from the raincoat in the pillowcase when the nurse came around to lock up her drawers and closets for the night. In the dark she had made a loop and tried to pull it tight around her throat. But always just as the air stopped coming and she felt the rushing grow louder in her ears, her hands would slacken and let go, and she would lie there panting for breath, cursing the dumb instinct in her body that fought to go on living." (*JPBD* 273)

In *The Bell Jar,* Esther Greenwood considers and experiments with strangulation as one possible form of suicide, trying a number of times before the final attempt with sleeping pills. At first, in her version of the scene, she hopes to hang herself, but finding no adequate beam in the house, she explains :

> "I sat on the edge of my mother's bed and tried pulling the cord tight. But each time I would get the cord so tight I could feel a rushing in my ears and a flush of blood in my face, my hands would weaken and let go and I would be all right again.
>
> Then I saw that body had all sorts of little tricks, such as making my hands go limp at the crucial second, which would save it, time and again whereas if I had the whole say, I would be dead in a flash." (*BJ* 130)

In this scene, the body's instinctual response is more malevolent; it is not simply 'dumb', but it has all sorts of little tricks. In *The Bell Jar,* the character's paranoia and mind-body split is strongly felt. The world is active in its oppression, the body active in its rebellion to the will.

Finally, both stories describe the insulin treatment used to combat the character's suicidal depressions. Each story starts with the appearance of a nurse to administer the insulin injection. In "Tongues of Stone" :

> At seven the nurse came in to give the evening insulin shot. What side? She asked, as the girl bent mechanically over the bed and barked flank. It does not matter, the girl said, "I cannot feel them anymore. The nurse gave an expert job. 'My your certainly are back and blue', she said" (*JPBD* 273-74).

In *The Bell Jar* the characters are both detached as well. The section is a little less calm, however, since we are at least aware of what Esther seen when she views herself.

> "The nurse gave a little clucking noise. Thus she said, 'which side?' It was an old joke. I raised my head and glanced back at my bare buttocks. They were bruised purple and green and blue from past injections. The left side looked darker than the right.
>
> 'The right.'
>
> 'You name it.' The nurse jabbed the needle in, and I winced, savoring the tiny hurt" (*BJ* 157).

It is also useful to note that Esther does feel something in this episode : pain. And that is welcomed, for it is something better than the dull apathy of the first scene.

The final movement in each story is the breakthrough caused by the girl's reactions to the insulin treatment in each case the reaction signals the momentary lifting of the oppressive atmosphere, the depression, and bell jar which each of the character is laboring under. After what has seemed a fruitless waiting in "Tongues of Stone", the girl's reaction occurs, accompanied by a proliferation of growth and light images.

> "In the blackness that was stupor that was sleep, a voice spoke to her, sprouting like a green plant in the dark.
>
> 'Mrs. Patterson, Mrs. Patterson, Mrs. Patterson!' the voice said more and more loudly, rising shouting. Light broke on seas of blindness. Air thinned.

> The nurse, Mrs. Patterson, came running out from behind the girl's eyes. 'Fine' she was saying, 'Fine. Let me just take off, your watch so you would not bang it on the bed.'
> 'Mrs. Patterson,' the girl heard herself say, 'Drink another glass of juice'. Mrs. Patterson was holding a white celluloid cup of orange juice to the girl's lips" (*JPBD* 274).

As the ending of the short story, this scene optimistically portends a healing conclusion. The sun has returned, in fact it is speaking directly to the girl. Both the blackness she emerges from and the real world represented by the nurse are positive, the first is the plant; the second, warm and round as an apple. The air is clear, the light quite literally and figuratively dawns. The girl herself speaks words and listens to a voice which apparently signals the start of a new world. *The Bell Jar* the parallel scene follows the same progression, but has a slightly different tone.

> "I had fallen as sleep after evening meal. I was awakened by a loud voice, Mrs. Bannister, Mrs. Bannister, Mrs. Bannister. As I pulled out of sleep, I found I was beating on the bedpost with my hands and calling. The sharp, way figure of Mrs. Bannister, the night nurse, scurried into view.
> 'Here, we do not want you to break this.'
> She unfastened the band of my watch.
> 'What is the matter? What happened?'
> Mrs. Bannister's face twisted into a quick smile.
> 'You have had reaction'.
> 'A reaction?'
> 'Yes, how do you feel?'
> 'Funny sort of light and airy.'
> Mrs. Bannister helped me sit up.
> 'You will be better now.
> You will better in no time.
> Would you like some hot milk?
> 'Yes.'
> And when Mrs. Bannister held the cup to my lips, I fanned the hot milk on my tongue as it went down,

tasting it luxuriously, the way a baby tastes its mother" (*DJ* 164).

In this scene, several things have changed. In "Tongues of Stone", the girl is the first one to focus on the change in both herself and her surroundings. She feels different and it is not just her. But the atmosphere, the world which is light and airy. In *The Bell Jar,* Esther feels 'funny', 'light and airy.' But we have no sense of whether external world is in accord. In "Tongues of Stone", the girl seems to have become attuned again to the physical, natural world. In *The Bell Jar* the natural world referred to is that of mother and child, not the most hopeful image when taken in the context of the heavily negative connotations given to that relationship throughout the rest of the novel, both before and after the scene. We really know that Esther's own relationship with her mother, her sense of all mothers — hers and Buddy's — as circumscribing her opportunities, the notion that becoming a mother herself would kill her chances to be writer, a complete person in her own right.

Really, Sylvia Plath, is using the same material, even some of the same phrases and images, in the early story and *The Bell Jar.* Equally obviously, there are some significant differences in her presentations, many of which seem caused by an increased thematic awareness on Plath's part in the novel. In "Tongues of Stone" we have more description than 'clearly delineated conflict. The causes of breakdown, the fears for the future, the active resistance of the girl to the both medical help and her surroundings, are never presented. It seems doubtful if the girl herself is aware of all the factors surroundings her previous actions. We are given third-person, limited view of the events. All conflicts and conditions leading to the suicide attempt are cloaked. In the expanded scope *The Bell Jar* on the other hand, the older Esther, the narrator, has moved to a recognition, frequently frustrated and angry, of the social and familial forces which lead to her breakdown. Her mother is seen in sharply critical relief. Her male doctor is at best indifferent to Esther's struggle; at worst he denies its value. It is a world of stultified options and intellectual sterility which please Esther under *The Bell Jar.* It is the thematic awareness even more than a stylistic change which gives *The Bell Jar* a power of lacking in the earlier story. This same factor accounts for much of the difference between the other apprentice pieces and the novel.

## WORKS CITED

Plath, Sylvia, *The Bell Jar.* London : Faber and Faber, 1966. Cited as *BJ.*

——, *Johny Panic and the Bible of Dreams.* London : Faber and Faber, 1979. Cited as *JPBD.*

# 5

# Philip Roth's *Goodbye, Columbus* : A Critique of American Philistinism

*—C.C. Mishra*

PHILIP ROTH exploded upon the American literary scene with the publication of his first novella *Goodbye, Columbus* in the year 1959. The book that won the National Book Award in 1960 and Darrof Award from the Jewish Book Council of America secured Roth's reputation in the literary circle ritually overnight. The *New York Times* hailed the twenty-six years old author as "A shrewd appraiser of a character and a keen recorder of an indecisive generation."

Roth has remained at the center of literary controversy for most of the succeeding years generating criticism ranging from perceptive to purely polemical. For combining a sharp eye for the middle class life style with an acid wit Roth's fictions are considered to be among the most poignant and sardonic of the postwar period. The Jewish core of his work, combined with his taste for satire led to the charges of anti-Semitism, a reaction which Roth typically enough parodied in many of his later works.

In the Preface of the novella *Goodbye, Columbus* Roth clearly articulates his stand in the following lines :

> "With clarity and with crudeness, and a great deal of exuberance, the embryonic writer who was me wrote these stories in his early twenties .... His cultural ambitions were formulated in direct opposition to the triumphant, suffocating American Philistinism of that time : he despised Time, Life, Hollywood, Television,

> The best seller list, advertising copy, Mc Carthyism, Rotary Clubs, Racial Prejudice and the American booster mentality" (Preface).

In short borrowing my cue from the author himself I would attempt a study of *Goodbye, Columbus* (the novella) as a critique of American Philistinism, asserting the Jews not only as a separate entity but also as a part of the American Populace.

The term "Philistintine" has been defined by *Webster's International Dictionary* (1992) as follows :

> "A person lacking liberal culture and refinement; one not appreciating the nobler aspirations and sentiments of humanity; a person especially of the middle class, who rejects enlightenment or is indifferent to the higher intellectual interests, preferring the material and commonplace; one whose scope is limited to selfish and material interests."

And *Oxford Illustrated Dictionary* (1998) defines it thus :

> "An illiberal person, one whose interests and tastes are material and commonplace, an uneducated or unenlightened person; a person indifferent or hostile to culture."

The term Philistinism in general means "an attitude of smug ignorance and conventionalism, especially towards artistic and cultural values." American Philistinism may be characterised by its pursuit of material prosperity, its business and money ethics superseding intellectual pursuit, its degrading value system both in the family and personal relationship such as love wherein body overrides the mind; its preference to food and club culture for bodily growth; over and above all these its rejection of traditional social, moral and religious values for the sake of a suburban material and commonplace living.

In *Goodbye, Columbus* Roth presents his views against American Philistinism through the protagonist Neil Klugman's first person narrative. He is a lower middle class Jewish boy from Newark, who has been working in the Newark library after having completed a course in Contemporary Moral Issues in the Newark College of Rutgers University. When the novella begins,

Neil is seen to have a summer affair with Brenda Patimkin, an affluent Jewish girl from suburban Short Hills, who is home on vacation from Radcliffe. It is through the narrator-hero Neil Klugman that the reader is intimated about the societal degradation and the moral depravity confronting the contemporary American milieu. By attributing special knowledge of contemporary moral issues to the hero the author ironically makes his intention clear enough for everybody to guess.

Neil Klugman is a representative of the present Jewish American society, who is yet to form any specific norm for life. His relationship, with Brenda is not the outcome of love rather a result of mutual sexual attraction. The sense of temporariness and impermanence pervading their relationship is too apparent also in Neil's attitude towards his job in the library. He is 'not a planner', so drifts through his love as well as his job with the same lack of commitment to permanency. Neil's parents have already left for Arizona due to their asthmatic health condition and poverty. Neil is left completely to himself to decide and shape his life according to the contemporary American ethic devoid of the protective parental moral influence to form his emotional, behavioural and intellectual growth.

A philistine is one who prefers the material and commonplace to the intellectual interests and one whose scope is limited to selfish and material interests. Neil Klugman at the age of twenty-three, is at the threshold of the American Dream of success where he must chose his next step to upward mobility either through his profession or through his human connection. Considering his job in the library and the immediate prospect if his being promoted to the reference section Neil calls it as 'muscleless devotion to my work.' It is obvious from his attitude that he would have much preferred a job requiring muscular exercise in stead of an intellectual one. Neil's parents belonged to the generation of 'work culture' who had remained poor throughout their lives. By changing his livelihood for the time being he may attempt to establish his identity but the American dream of material prosperity is already seeded in his mind. As he yet to take a decision his initial reaction after meeting Brenda is :

> "...and so life from now on would be not a throwing off, as it was for Aunt Gladys; and not a gathering in, as it was for Brenda; but a bouncing off, a numbness" (23).

Neil's first step towards 'bouncing off" is to have the affluent Jewish girl Brenda whose parents have given up their Newark ethnic life for suburban Short Hills life of material prosperity. The relationship between Neil and Brenda from its very origin is devoid of any moral or intellectual base. Mutual sexual attraction forms the core of their love, it is through such a nexus that Neil attempts to climb the "hundred and eighty feet that make summer nights so much cooler in Short Hills than in Newark."

In his venture of the American Dream Neil finds himself attracted to the Patimkin house, that Allan Cooper calls "a paradise of sex without responsibility." After having sex with Brenda, Neil's initial aggressiveness of social climbing becomes tinged with envy. When he thinks of proposing marriage to her, for the first time he could only suggest her to acquire a diaphragm. Though Brenda shows her reluctance, she succumbs to him only for his personal pleasure. The second time he considers proposing to her when he visits her in Boston, he is shocked to know that her mother has already discovered the diaphragm in her drawer at home. Neil's dream for a paradise of sex without responsibility is shattered. He has already encountered the frightened insecurity of Brenda during her angry rivalry with her mother and made love to her in the attic at her demand. Neil is too powerless to override her aggressive acquisitiveness. So instead of comforting, her, he prefers to walk out of the impermanent bond.

Neil the narrator-hero is quite bitter about the obsessive food culture and the eating habits of the Patimkins both on the paternal and the maternal side. All of them are victims of over eating and talk of cheap irrelevant day to day affairs too mundane and gross in their nature.

> "Their was not much dinner conversation; eating was heavy and methodical and serious, and it would be just as well to record all that was said in one swoop, rather than indicate the sentences lost in the passing of food, the words gurgled into mouthfuls the syntax chopped and forgotten in heapings, spillings, and gorgings" (15).

The Patimkins are the exemplers of the American Dream come true. Their refrigerator is stuffed with fruits.

> "Fruit grew in their refrigerator" (31).

Their house is big and spacious, where each member is virtually separated from the other. Their store room full of old furniture may remind them of their roots in Newark but it fails to remind them of their Jewish values. According to the philistine American idealism they have 'made it'. All their children's posh education, and nose fixing has failed to save their intimate family relationship. Ronald's marriage only provides them another opportunity to show off their indulgence without insistence on any moral sense.

> "There was Mrs. Patimkin's side of the family : his sister Molly, a tiny buxom hen whose ankles swelled and ringed her shoes, and who would remember Ron's wedding if for no other reason than she'd martyred her feet in three inch heels, and Molly's husband, the butter and egg man, Harry Grosbart, who had earned his fortune with barley and corn in the days of prohibition. Now he was active in the temple and whenever he saw Brenda he swatted her on the can; it was a kind of physical boot legging that passed, I guess, for familial affection. Then there was Mrs. Patimkin's brother, Marty Kreiger, the Kosher Hot-Dog King, an immense man, as many stomachs as he had chins and already at fifty with as many heart attacks as chins and stomachs combined. He had just come back from a health care in the Catskills, where he said he'd eaten nothing but All-Bran and had won $ 1500 at gin rummy. When the photographer came by to take pictures, Marty put his hand on his wife's pancake breasts, and said 'Hey, how about a picture of this?' " (75)

In the words of Dan Isaac the whole description above

> "is a satiric demonstration of how the house of modern Judaism rests on a base of vulgar and mindless materialism. Ron Patimkin's wedding gives us an entire gallery of the nouveaux riches."

I do agree to Dan Isaac's views but would like to add that what Roth is concerned here is not only with Judaism but go beyond to suggest that Patimkin's are more close to their Christian counterpart by emulating the ways of the Protestant upper-class.

Says George Santayana,

> "A philistine may be religious in his gregarious way, his faith may be orthodox and his conduct irreproachable but he lacks instinctive piety and an inward, imaginative appreciation of his faith."

Roth targets the American milieu, especially the Jews only because he feels more at home with them. They have made it to the suburbs of American Dream only by shedding their religious and ethical values for a material and carnal pursuit. Jewish holidays do not heighten the reverence for Jewish values rather they turn into opportunities for licentiousness. Rosh Ha-Shonah is merely a chance for Neil to get off work and go to Boston to continue his sexual romance with Brenda. It is equally pathetic to observe Mrs. Patimkin's senseless talks about orthodox and liberal followers of Judaism and her ignorance about philosopher like Martin Buber. What more to talk of her membership of Hadassah which was founded to widen and deepen the awareness among Jews in America, of Jewish traditions and ideals. Neil is as much a pagan as Mrs. Patimkin is smug and ignorant.

It is due to these deep and inbred criticism of the Jewish life that Roth incurred the Rabbinical attack time and again. In the journal *To Our Colleagues* published in summer 1964 writes Rabbi Saul I. Taplitz :

> "Philip Roth, of 'Good Bye, Columbus' fame, constantly depicts the Jewish characters in his short stories and novels as depraved and lecherous creatures.... The only

> logical conclusion any intelligent reader could draw from his stories or books that this country — nay that the world — would be a much better and happier place without Jews."

The purpose of quoting these comments is not to refute them. Rather I am inclined to believe that the Rabbi's outburst had a grain of truth in them. Yet looking at them from the novelist's point of view it would be better if we understand Rabbi's 'this country without Jews' to mean the America without the Philistines.

The Philistines are more engrossed with their physical development and bodily satisfaction. The whole Patimkin family stands for these fallen virtues of American Dream. Ron and Brenda drive golf balls, play tennis and go for swimming. It is during swimming that Neil enjoys Brenda's virginal lush body. Mr. Patimkin and his youngest daughter Julie are always seen playing some game or the other. Neil sarcastically enough describes his impression in the following manner :

> "Outside; through the wide picture window, I could see the back lawn with its twin oak trees. I say oaks, though fancifully, one might call them sporting goods trees. Beneath their branches, like fruit dropped from their limbs, were two irons, a golf ball, a tennis can, a base ball bat, basket ball, a first-baseman's glove, and what was apparently a riding crop" (15).

In addition to this the Patimkins attempt to assimilate in the main stream American life by fixing their noses to hide the bumps of their Jewish birth pushes them forward into the Philistine class. Even the education of their children in famous universities life the Ohio State University ends their intellectual pursuit in the "General Store of Patimkin Kitchen and Bathroom Sinks."

For a society nurturing the motto of thriving through money and business, its children have to make do with the nostalgia of Home-coming game and bidding good bye to all such memories once they are out of them. It may be pointed out here that

Brenda's Radcliffe enrolment nowhere in the novella gives any impression of her having a head or any trace of intellectuality. Roth, it appears, is inclined to suggest that the so-called institutes of learning too cannot serve their aim of inspiring the contemporary Jewish American youth for a higher ideal of life.

It is in the dream sequence that Roth is able to exclude the exclusiveness of his attack on the Jewish community alone. In the dream Neil finds himself and the Negro boy, who visited the library to watch the sensual Gauguin paintings in a moving boat but he was unable to do anything to stop it. Neil and the Negro boy are representative of the two different race of American society trying to follow respectively the journey to upward mobility. Neil has already seen the emptiness of Patimkins' values. Now Brenda has to choose between her parents who equate love with money and Neil who can offer occasional sex in the name of love. She chooses her parents, thereby Neil's further move into the posh corridor of Patimkin Philistine life comes to an end. At the same time by debarring the black boy from watching the sensual painting Roth seems to suggest that his cycle of satire is complete. Finally, Neil is left alone to "look hard at his image." "He begins his journey back to Newark, which has positive implications for his finally beginning to make some order of his life."

Finally, it would be apt to judge Roth's success as a critic of American Philistinism in the light of the comment made by George Santayana, a Spanish philosopher in his essay "What is a Philistine?" :

> "It matters not what the sacred passion or what the work of love may be : the infinite surrounds us in every direction, and all who have caught a glimpse of it have something in common. They have for a moment escaped convention and felt the relativity and possible indifference of, all earthly goods. That is what the Philistine has never done. He has never shaken off his vulgar passions nor felt the weight of original sin; his life like that of a beast of burden, has not been either a revel or a sacrifice, but a stolid response to successive stimulations."

In *Goodbye, Columbus* all characters have some such fallibilities which inevitably point at each one's Philistinic identity. Neither thc Patimkins, nor the Narrator-hero Neil Klugman, nor the Negro boy shows or show any sign of possessing the sacred passion to appreciate the values of a higher life. Almost all of them have given into their physical stimulations. Roth has quite successfully presented these representative characters of American society in life and blood. Concluding with the words of George Santayana would be the best way to judge the author in the best perspective :

> "However narrow a life may be, however ignorant of the wide world of nature and thought, if it is governed by some true perception, or it has hold upon some immediate and vital good, it escapes conventionally."

All is not lost in this conventional material world. Rothvian Narrator-Hero Neil Klugman does show the sign of beginning a new order by defying the conventionality through his rejection of Patimkin world.

## WORKS CITED

Isaac, Dan, "In Defence of Roth". *Critical Essays on Philip Roth*. Ed. Sanford Pinsker. Boston : G.K. Hall & Co., 1982.

Jones, Judith Patterson and Guineverra A. Nance, *Philip Roth*. np. Frederic Unger Publishing Co., Inc., 1981.

Lyon, Rochard Colton, ed., *Santayana on American*. An Original Harbinger Book, Harcourt, Brace & World, Inc., 1968.

Roth, Philip, *Goodbye, Columbus and Five Short Stories*. New York : Nentam Books, Inc., 1970.

# 6

# Hemingway, the Feminist

*—Susheela Beniwal*

ERNEST HEMINGWAY (1899-1961), popularly known as 'Papa Hemingway', has been synonymous with a stereotype of masculinity. Thus it is that in the feminist reading of his fiction the accusation of male chauvinism and misogyny hangs large over the man and his work. His early stories were greatly played up by the related canon, and won remarkable critical acclaim for their understated masculine style and minute and accurate depiction of male pursuits and attitudes. A brief survey of Hemingway criticism only exposes its excessive concern with Hemingway the legendary masculine figure. Robert P. Weeks admits as much, and observes that "his [Hemingway's] personal legend has seized our imagination as firmly as his novels and stories." One of the aspects of Hemingway's work which has not been given due attention is his deft management of identity crisis by his women characters. There is a false assumption that Hemingway neglects his female characters and reduces them to mere props incidental to the story, and that his fiction is, in the final analysis, male-oriented. Out of this assumption, some early male critics manhandle his striking women characters and ignore those which he creates with sensitivity to the woman's point of view. For such critics Brett Ashley of *The Sun Also Rises* is a Circe (Spilka 20-29) who turned men into swine. Catherine Barkley of *A Farewell to Arms*, a divine lollipop (Hatchett 32), and the female protagonists of the African stories "American bitches of the most soul-destroying sort" (Wilson). Before looking into Hemingway's much-maligned women and examining the nature and significance of their identity crisis, it will be rewarding to review the existing critical responses to Hemingway's work in this context.

Hemingway's seminal critics of the nineteen-thirties, such as Max Eastman (McCaffery 59), Wyndham Lewis and Delmore Schwartz (McCaffery 114-29), in their criticism, project Hemingway as an author preoccupied with masculine themes of physical courage and stoic death. He is made out by them to be a demi-god of few words — a dumb ox. They highlight the masculinity in his writings. Max Eastman, in his notorious review "Bull in the Afternoon," debunks Hemingway's masculine posturing as "a wearing of false hair on the chest." His early stories are lauded for their masculine style and graphic depiction of male pursuits and attitudes. It is even believed that Hemingway is working deliberately to develop and embellish a masculine public image of himself (Raeburn). Keeping up the current trend, Ivan Keshkeen insists that, in crating his characters, including the female ones, Hemingway is writing of the end of everything — love, life and hope. A close reading of his works, however, reveals exactly the opposite. While his contemporaries visualize woman only as demi-goddesses, or bitches, Hemingway, as a true feminist, portrays his women as human beings, as passing through the same traumas and crisis as men, and as emerging equally heroic, if not more, with them. Hemingway's female protagonists share, as much as men, the characteristics of the Hemingway hero in general as specified by Dahiya :

> The heroism of this character is not a matter of physical courage, nor of a personal success in a dangerous situation; it is characterized by his larger concern for the fate of human society, by his complex awareness of life and by his mental courage that shows itself in withstanding stresses and strains of his complex awareness.

In the forties, with the publication of Hemingway's new works, most critics compare his fiction of the twenties with that of the forties. Maxwell Geismar discovers in Hemingway's protagonists in his later works a movement from separatism to social commitment. Hemingway's leading characters are searched for depth in the human material. Malcolm Cowley suggests that Hemingway has greater affinity with symbolists like Poe, Hawthorne and Melville. It is in the forties that Edmund Wilson, an early admirer of Hemingway, first discerns and criticizes a growing antagonism to women in Hemingway's works.

Nineteen-fifties offer a number of full-length studies of Hemingway's works, all of them based on the biographical approach. There being a close affinity between Hemingway and his heroes, it is commonly assumed that the novelist puts a great deal of himself into his protagonists. According to Philip Young, Hemingway wrote so that he could get rid of certain emotions, and sometimes learn to live with them. Carlos Baker believes that the Hemingway hero is an autobiographical figure. Like Young, he also upholds the concept of code hero. Charles A. Fenton is wholly biographical in the perspective. For John W. Aldridge both Hemingway and his heroes are products of the 'lost generation.'

Nineteen-sixties offer a variety of viewpoints. Though the chief concern continues to be a biographical interpretation of Hemingway's works, Robert William Lewis' psychological study reiterates the critical view that writing fiction gave Hemingway psychic relief. Lewis goes on to say that Hemingway's own problems are reflected in the portraits of his protagonists. Carlos Baker, in his official biography, *Ernest Hemingway : A Life Story*, shows how Hemingway was writing a series of sketches of his own life. Stewart Sanderson, and Earl Rovit accept Young's view of the Hemingway hero and the code hero, though with a changed rhetoric in different novels. John Killinger offers a philosophical view in his *Hemingway and the Dead Gods : A Study in Existentialism*. He asserts that Hemingway's characters involve themselves in adventures because they have gone through the trauma of death and must continually recreate it. Cleanth Brooks offers a social perspective when he says that the Hemingway hero tries to establish himself as a man in a dehumanized world. Sheridan Baker's *Ernest Hemingway : An*

*Introduction and Interpretation* considers the heroes in Hemingway to be distinct and independent of the author. Richard Peterson's *Hemingway : Direct and Oblique* concerns itself with Hemingway's style. Jackson J. Benson's *Hemingway : The Writer's Art of Self-Defense* looks into the difference between Hemingway's early and later heroes. One significant work which looks beyond biography, and distinguishes Hemingway the man from his fictional protagonists is Delbert E. Wylder's study *Hemingway's Heroes*. During the 1960s Hemingway's women were given some attention. A great deal of Hemingway criticism during this period was, however, unfortunately written under the influence of Leslie Fiedler's *Love and Death in the American Novel* (1960), a tremendously popular critical work suggesting that American literature, in its entirety, could be interpreted as an elaboration of the idea that the only good woman is a dead one. Besides, probably the dearth of women critics during 1960 is also responsible for the negative critical reputation of Hemingway. Only a few women appear as 'second authors' with their husbands or male colleagues in the early sixties. Only one woman critic, a graduate student, dares to challenge the existing male-oriented criticism, and discuss female characters in Hemingway's fiction. Hemingway's death in 1961 marks an explosion of biographies by his family and friends, the more significant works being Alfred G. Aronowitz and Peter Hammils' *Ernest Hemingway : The Life and Death of a Man*, Kurt D. Singer's *Hemingway : Life and Death of a Giant* and Milt Machlin's *The Private Hell of Ernest Hemingway*, Leicester Hemingway's *My Brother, Ernest Hemingway*, Marcelline Hemingway Sanford's *At the Hemingways : A Family Portrait* and A.E. Hotchner's *Papa Hemingway*.

The criticism in the seventies offers a break from the monotony of a single approach. Floyd C. Watkins makes a comparative study of Eliot, Hemingway and Faulkner, Michael S. Reynolds dwells on the background of World War I as leading to the making of *A Farewell to Arms*. Arthur Waldheen is not very different from Young when he substitutes the apprentice here for the autobiographical hero. The protagonist is equated with Hemingway and both are shown struggling to form an identity. Linda Wagner considers Hemingway primarily as an imagist. Another unconventional Hemingway critic is Sheldon N. Grebstein, who considers humour as one of Hemingway's prime virtues. According to Malcolm Bradbury and David Palmer, Hemingway modeled his heroes on three roles — those of the sportsman, the soldier-of-fortune and the journalist. Chaman Nahal deals with Hemingway's narrative technique in his *The Narrative Patterns in Ernest Hemingway*. Bhim S. Dahiya, in *The Hero in Hemingway : A Study in Development* discards the theory of two separate heroes — the code hero and the Hemingway hero — and traces the growth of the hero in Hemingway's works. Emily Stipes Watts offers an interdisciplinary approach when she traces the influence of painting, sculpture and architecture in Hemingway's works.

During 1970s one factor which is dominant in Hemingway criticism is a constitutional amendment known as ERA (Equal Rights Amendment), prohibiting gender discrimination against women. Hemingway's works already seen from Philip Young's viewpoint of entirely finding in them "what makes a man a man" are now reviewed to also consider what makes a woman a woman. The revival of feminism is seen having an immediate and positive impact on Hemingway studies. Pamella Farley's "From and Function : The Image of woman in selected works of Hemingway and Fitzgeralds, "Deborah Fischer's "Genuine Heroines : Hemingway Style," Janet Lynne Pearson's "Hemingway Women" and Sunita Jain's "Of Women and Bitches : Two Hemingway Heroines Exonerated" challenge the male critics' assumption. Women scholars are not always complimentary to Hemingway. Judith Fetterley's *A Farewell to Arms : Hemingway's Resentful Cryptogram* remains one of the best known feminist assaults on what has been thought the author's hostility to women. By 1978 there are even hints of a backlash when William Spofford publishes his "*Beyond the Feminist Perspective : Love in A Farewell to Arms*."

Even in the early eighties Hemingway criticism continues to be overshadowed by the conventional biographical approach. Compared to the sixties and seventies, there are fewer complete studies of Hemingway's work published in this decade. Apart from a biography by Kenneth Lynn, there are only studies of the individual novels. Frederick J. Svaboda in his *Hemingway and The Sun Also Rises*, takes up Jake Barnes in *The Sun Also Rises*. It is stressed that the understanding of Hemingway's aesthetics is necessary to fully understand the various levels of meaning in his works.

In the early eighties, when French deconstruction is much in vogue in literary circles, Hemingway criticism suffers a setback. In the late eighties with the birth of feminist criticism, the focus shifts to Hemingway's women at the hands of women critics. Hemingway's alleged misogyny comes under fierce attack of feminist critics. Many of these critics focus on rehabilitating Hemingway for feminist readers — on making him "correct." There are Linda W. Wagner's "Proud and Friendly and Gently : Women in Hemingway's Early Fiction", Joyce Wexler's "ERA for Hemingway : A Feminist Defense of *A Farewell to Arms*," Sandra Spanier's "Catherine Barkley and the Hemingway Code : Ritual and Survival in *A Farewell to Arms*," Mimi Reisel Gladstein's *The Indestructible Woman in Faulkner, Hemingway and Steinbeck* and Pamela Smiley's "Gender-Linked Miscommunication in 'Hills Like White Elephants.' " Some male critics like Charles J. Nolan also participate in the movement. Mark Spilka's essay "Hemingway and Faunteroy : An Androgynous Pursuit" and Gerry Brenner's psycho-analytic study *Concealments in Hemingway's Works* (1983) attack Hemingway's facade of hyper-masculinity which they set about dismantling with psychoanalytic tools. To Spilka, Hemingway's emphatic assertion of masculinity is part of a larger struggle with his own androgynous impulses.

In late eighties and early nineties, complete studies of Hemingway's women come up. Studies of gender relationship, as, for instance, during 1920s, mark Hemingway criticism.

Dorothy N. Brown looks at the women of 1920s as the predecessors of recent feminists. Kert Bernice offers a full-length study of Hemingway's women. Linda Patterson Miller re-assesses Hemingway's women. Carol H. Smith looks into Hemingway's women from a mythical context. He argues that the charge of androgyny and the feminists' quarrel with Hemingway for misrepresenting women are baseless. The publication of Hemingway's posthumously published novel *The Garden of Eden* in 1986 constitutes another landmark in Hemingway studies. Now in Hemingway criticism the "wound theory" (Wilson) and the code hero theory (Dahiya) are replaced by the "theory of androgyny" (Spilka, Brenner). With this theory, Hemingway's façade of hyper-masculinity comes under attack. For Spilka, Hemingway's "Strenuous defense of maleness becomes part of a larger struggle with his own androgynous impulses." According to Brenner, "Beneath his [Hemingway's] masculine swagger lay puerile diffidence. An advocate of courage, he was fear-ridden." Kenneth Lynn interprets Hemingway's life and work exclusively in the light of the author's "androgyny" and "sexual confusion", which Lynn views as the result of Mrs. Hemingway's dressing toddler Ernest in baby clothes identical to his older sister's.

Hemingway's works have been studied in androgynous light (Lynn, Brenner, Spilka & Kert). It is however discovered in the course of the present study that the change of androgyny, and that of misrepresenting women, against Hemingway are misplaced, that the novelist judges his men and women by the same yardstick. This may be read as both a virtue and a fault. Thus, Tom Burnam makes out that Hemingway's women are simply Hemingway's men only slightly and superficially altered, and that since Hemingway has the same stockbin of virtue for both the sexes, he has failed to create a distinct set of values for women.

Hemingway offers a fairly realistic portrayal of the women around him. His women are no mere exact replicas of the individuals in his life, but rather products of a creative writer suiting his fancy as prompted by the spirit of his time. These women do mostly come from autobiographical sources, and can, to some extent, reveal the cultural clime of his time. Grace Hall Hemingway, the author's mother, was a deeply religious and strictly puritan lady, and had an overbearing influence on the family. She was a strict disciplinarian, and whenever Hemingway used a vulgar word, she made him wash his mouth with soap solution. In his mother, Hemingway had a prototype of the domineering type of woman. She overruled his father and subjected him to her own whim and temper. She exercised authority over him, never brooking any opposition or surrendering her own self-will. Hemingway once openly characterized his mother as "a domineering shrew" who drove his father to suicide (Baker *SL* 670).

During his Paris years, Hemingway came into contact with Gertrude Stein, who proved to be one of his literary gurus. In his apprenticeship of the craft of writing he is greatly influenced by this litterateur. To him, she is a sort of literary mother, and he holds her in high esteem. He writes to his friend Anderson in March 1922, "Gertrude Stein and me are just like brothers" (Baker 352). The statement is pertinent in an age when men are highly sceptical about women and hold them in low esteem. He admires Stein to the extent of calling her his 'brother', and hence worthy of attention and admiration. By the twenties, there is already developed the concept of the modern woman, which combines the flapper's physical freedom, sexuality and stamina with the feminist self-assertiveness and traditional domestic femininity (Schneider). In keeping with the current trend, Hemingway is attracted towards the new female ideal. All his wives are independent young women — Hadley Richardson has inherited a modest trust fund, and hence has a steady income; Martha Gellhorn is a writer; and his last wife, Mary Welsh, is a news woman. All his wives have a wide interest in sports. Hadley likes hiking and skiing; Pauline is good at riding and shooting; Martha loves hunting; and Mary is an expert deep-sea fisherwoman. What is more, during his youth, his most serious relationship involve older, more mature women. Gertrude Stein, the nurse Agnes Von Kurowsky, his first wife, Hadley, Duff Twysden (the model for Brett Ashley) and his second wife Pauline are all several years senior to him.

As regards Hemingway's response to the cultural and intellectual scene, he was well aware of the Freudian thought and the women's liberation from Victorian sexual taboos that it promoted. Though it is uncertain whether Hemingway actually read Freud, it is known that in 1920 and 1921 he read and recommended to his friends the voluminous *Studies in Psychology* by serologist-cum-philosopher Havelock Ellis. He sent three volumes of it to Hadley, and they exchanged notes on the topic (Reynolds).

Besides, feminism as a movement greatly affected Hemingway. In Post-War Paris, among the expatriates feminism was most prevalent — there were over eighty feminist societies, representing more than sixty thousand members (Martin 65-82). During his Paris years, Hemingway encountered many of these female feminists. Hemingway's position as an apprentice writer surrounded by these women probably explains the important challenge posed to him by feminists. His response to the bohemian and sexually permissive environment that the feminist movement induced was ambivalent. Although he derided the hypocritical narrow-mindedness of the patriarchal gender relations (*SL* Baker), he also condemned promiscuity (Donaldson). Turning away from the sexual anarchy of the times, Hemingway adopted a kind of philosophical primitivism. In this he was not alone. T.S. Eliot's "The Waste Land" (1922) and Oswald Spengler's *The Decline of the West* (1918) undertook a quest for the essential values that the modern civilization, in their view, had abandoned. Some critics go to the extent of regarding "The Waste Land" to be the source of *The Sun Also Rises*.

In his Paris years, living as an expatriate amongst the intelligentsia of the age, Hemingway attempted to understand the changing social fabric in his trilogy *The Sun Also Rises* (1926), *A Farewell to Arms* (1929) and *For Whom the Bell Tolls* (1940).

*The Sun Also Rises* deals with the changing attitude to women. The American women experienced a widening of their spheres of interest and activity due to the peculiar circumstances of 1920s juxtaposed with the prevalent myths of the American hero as a success prodigy and the victorian tradition of the genteel woman. This attempt to understand the new woman is not new in American literature. In the American literature, the first well-known new woman is Hester Pyrnne in Nathaniel Hawthorne's *The Scarlet Letter*. Her infidelity conflicts directly with the rigid puritan codes of the society of Hawthorne's time. By 1890s such a figure had become common in American literature. Celia Madden in Harold Frederic's *The Damnation of Theron Ware* and Edna Pontellier in Stephen Crane's *Maggie* are women who design their own code of conduct, which is, a code that is free of the prescribed gender roles and the restraints of the traditional society. The 19th century authors drew a censoring portrait of these women. However, by the turn of the century there was a marked change of authorial attitude. The disapproval of the author was replaced by understanding, and even sympathy. In *Sister Carrie*, a novel based closely on the life of his sister, Theodore Dresier created Carrie Meeber, who lives with a man without marriage, leaves him for another man, and then deserts him too when her career as an actress in New York is well established. She does so without authorial condemnation or overt punishment. In the context of these earlier women in American literary history, the "new woman" of Hemingway is not dramatically new character.

Hemingway's short stories of *In Our Time* (1925) paved the way for his novels. The Nick Adams stories register as much the author's as Nick's initiation into the feminine world. In these stories there is the feminist world in its infancy there is a progressive development of women's identity from "Indian Camp" to "The End of Something." In "Indian Camp", woman is the object of patriarchy — things happen to her. Since she fails in her traditional role of procreation, she is forced to perform it by undergoing a caesarian section. In "The Doctor and the

Doctor's Wife" the woman, symbolically a social artifact, tries to impose restrictions on Nick and his father but fails. In "Ten Indians" two sets of gender roles are juxtaposed together, those of the traditional patriarchy with the reversed ones. In the Garnes household, the lady of the house is shown building a fire in the stove, but in Adamse's Kitchen it is the father who brings the boy a piece of cold chicken. In the story "The End of Something", Hemingway questions the very basis of gender roles. Marjorie vies with Nick for assuming the traditional masculine role. By performing the masculine role better than Nick, Marjorie demonstrates that these characteristics do not come automatically to any male or female. Hence, what is understood to be masculine/feminine distinction is a social artifact. The idea implied is similar to Simone de Beauvoir's — that "one is not born a woman but becomes one." With "The Cat in the Rain" the focus shifts entirely to women. In the story Catherine's yearning to break away from patriarchal entrapment realistically reflects the general predicament of women in Hemingway's time, and the dilemma that she faces is typical of that faced by women in that time. She wants the security of patriarchy as well as the adventure of being a new woman. The desire and attempt to sort out gender relations is the binding thread running through all these stories.

The men of the modern era were haunted by a new kind of femme fatale — the flapper, with her short skirts and bobbed hair, her feverish dancing, wild drinking and wilful wandering like Brett Ashley of *The Sun Also Rises* (1926). The flapper was a phenomenon that came just upon Daisy Buchanan of F. Scott. Fitzgerald's *The Great Gatsby* (1925). In Brett Ashley, Hemingway is contradicting Fitzgerald's narcissistic Daisy, who incarnates the corrupted morals of society. Daisy's destructive power reaches a climax when she casually slams her lovers expensive automobile in her husband's mistress in a hit-and-run accident. This eventually leads not only to the woman's death, but also later to the deaths of the two men. Contrasted with Daisy, Brett Ashley proves not to be a flapper at all. She is haunted by her defiance, and is overcome by qualms in the end, as against Daisy, who could not care less. The flapper having been left behind, in Brett Ashley the new woman is in birth pangs. The problem with the new woman is that she has rejected absolute patriarchy but has no new role model to emulate. The new woman wants to emulate the masculine ways because they symbolize power, but, on close contact, she finds men equally weak and impotent (like Jake). So, Brett the new woman remains more an object of sympathy than contempt.

In the original opening of the novel, which was left out in the published version on the advice of F. Scott Fitzgerald, Hemingway had given an even more sympathetic treatment to Brett (Martin 239-47). In it the author had given her parents and a background — a sense of roots — which is missing in the printed version. She was introduced sympathetically, as a victim of psychological damage. But in the printed version, the sympathy for her is played down, it being almost the end of the book before the reader discovers that Brett is thirty-four and has suffered a massive psychological trauma. It is only towards the end that it is discovered that she has lost her true love in war and suffered abuse by her husband, Ashley. He slept with a loaded service revolver, and she had to defend herself by taking the shells out when he was asleep (*SAR* 169). When the book opens, this patriarchal oppression is already a thing of the past, and Brett is getting a divorce. Before ushering in Brett, the structure of the then man-woman relations is revealed : we have Cohn's passivity versus France's dynamism (*SAR* 6) divorces (*SAR* 10), live-in relations aimed at financial security of women (*SAR* 7), lack of romance (*SAR* 10), sexual perversions, impotence and prostitution (*SAR* 15). In this topsy-turvy world, romance is lost, yet, romance, family and love — all evoke an element of nostalgia in the characters of the lost generation. Jake remembers that as he took his evening stroll on the Notre Dame bridge, a man and a girl passed him. They were walking romantically, with their arms around each other. Hemingway must have thought it important to incorporate this reminder of courtship and romance in the printed version for the passage does not figure in the original manuscript (Facsimile Edition 222). At the end of the book too, in spite of all that has taken place, there is a hint of romance : "Oh, Jake", Brett said, "We could have had such a damned good time together." Ahead was a mounted policeman in khaki directing traffic. He raised his batón. The car slowed suddenly, pressing Brett against me. 'Yes', I said, 'Isn't it pretty to think so?" (*SAR* 206)

In the novel Jacques Barnes serves as the omniscient narrator, and Brett, following the picaresque tradition, moves from one adventure to another. While looking at the novel from a feminist viewpoint, it is important to observe that the whole novel is a narrative confession by Jake Barnes, who is free to tell what pleases him and delete what does not. What is more, he is narrating in retrospect, after evaluating the incidents from his own viewpoint, and hence objectivity cannot be expected in his narration, and one has to superimpose objectivity on his tainted version to get the correct picture.

In the very first chapter, along with sexual liberation is introduced the new woman's wish for independence and career :

> 'You are very nice people', he said. He was smoking a cigar again. "Why don't you get married, you two:"
> "We want to lead our own lives," I said.
> "We have our careers," Brett said. (*SAR* 52)

For the new woman her sexual liberation is one way of affirming her identity. Apparently, the story is Jake's confession, yet the heroic discovery takes place only in Brett's psyche. It is her endeavour to come to terms with what has happened, to pick up the threads of life and begin life afresh with what remains which binds the novel together.

Sheridan Baker regards Brett as a personification of sex without responsibility : the siren. Even when there is no dearth of critics who condemn Brett in all possible ways (say Spilka), it has to be admitted that in spite of her nymphomania, which is more a source of torment to her than to others, she is aware of the ruinous effects of promiscuity. Her remorses tells about her dilemma which is no less than Hamlet's. Brett verges on being a new woman (rather than a flapper) but she lacks comprehensiveness. Her tentative efforts deal with only one aspect of liberation : sexual indulgence. She is a transitional figure between the protected and idealized wife and the modern self-reliant woman. Although there is no formal alliance of matrimony, Brett and Jake share a husband-wife-like relationship. Brett feels bound to confess to Jake all her exploits. Patriarchal security is sought by her. Whenever she is in trouble she calls Jake for help. She lacks financial independence, which should go with her being a new woman. There is no consideration of procreation in her sexual relations. Brett and the women of her age are too aware of their sexuality which they see as a symbol of a new-found power. The traditional sexual roles are inverted with female aggression and male passivity. The encounter between Brett and Romero serves as a point of reference for these new gender relations. The encounter between Brett and Romero is a clash of patriarchy and feminist freedom. Romero's demand that Brett should grow her hair is a demand to adhere to the tenets of patriarchy; as it would make her "more womanly". But her encounter with Romero serves as a moment of epiphany for Brett, and transforms her from a flapper to a new woman. The metamorphosis takes place with her realisation that promiscuity is not the answer to the modern question of meaning of life, and hence her heroic decision to halt it immediately, so that the new generation is not tainted by it, and can seek its own answers. The episode further has a cathartic effect after which rising above her own selfish interest, she protects Romero's interest — almost working out the mother role of seeing to the child's welfare. Hemingway further suggests that the changes in the new woman are irrevocable. When confronted with the choice of patriarchy and feminist independence, Brett chooses independence, and decides against marrying Romero, because Romero is an old-fashioned man and would expect his wife to be a traditional woman. But, Brett realises that she cannot go back in time. She makes the momentous decision not to destroy the future generations. She decides not to be "one of those bitches that ruin children." On her part her decision not to pass on her malaise to the next generation is heroic :

> 'You know I feel rather damned, good Jake.'
> 'You should.'
> 'You know it makes one fell rather good deciding not to be a bitch.'
> 'Yes.'
> 'It's a sort of what we have instead of God.' (*SAR* 205)

Once she decides not to meddle with Romero, Brett feels good, almost godly. The decision is difficult, and she does not want to be reminded of it : "I won't be one of those bitches, but, oh Jake, please let's never talk about it." (*SAR* 205)

Hemingway's verdict on the situation is optimistic. He suggests that in spite of everything it is not the end of the world and the search for something better must continue :

> "You ought to dream," Bill said, "All our biggest businessmen have been dreamers. Look at Ford, Rockefeller or to Davidson." (*SAR* 103)

Contrasted with the notion of the flapper is that of femininity. Hemingway shares the prevalent masculine expectations of a woman that she should be tender, gentle and full of graces. She should be entirely self-effacing in her devotion to her men, reaching her greatest happiness in losing her identity in that of her male counterpart. Hemingway's Catherine, Marie and Renata are all attempts to create this ideal of womanhood, similar to Yeats' in his "A Prayer for My Daughter" (1919). Some critics have charged that these women are unreal (Cowley 46). But, the motive in all these attempts is not realism, but an attempt to transcend time and space, looking for universality and ideal probability. It is as if true femininity rises sphinx like from the ashes of the flapper.

Catherine Barkley of the next novel of the triology, *A Farewell to Arms*, has been the butt of disapproval by critics. She has been called "old fashioned — not a new woman," (Bardacke 345) "a divine lollipop" (Hatchett), and "a leaf of lettuce" (Cooperman 185). But, these charges are not justified, because her strong individuality, independent thinking and philosophical views emerge into bold relief, highlighting the solidity and sturdy concreteness of her personality. In a cosmopolitan gathering, Catherine has been given a British nationality — a symbol of tradition. Before introducing her, the prevalent gender relations are made known. Women are just "girls" of the whore house. When Catherine appears she has already suffered considerable trauma. She is a disillusioned romantic. Her childhood beau has died in war, and she carries his "thin rotten stick," which was delivered to her as a souvenir after his death. In a way, she has not been able to overcome her past. She had romantic notions about love and war. She did not marry her childhood love, waiting for a suitable opportunity when the wedding could be picturesque enough. About war, she had a dream of playing nurse to her chivalrous knight-in-armour : "I remember having a silly idea that he might come to the hospital, where I was with a sabre cut, I suppose, and a bandage around his head or a shot through the shoulder, something picturesque" (*FA* 19).

She was disillusioned by the mundane nature of war. Her fiance was blown to pieces and there was nothing heroic about it. Now, in an atmosphere where "anybody may crack", she has cracked. Breaking down, she pleads with Henry : "Oh Darling," she said, "You will be good to me, won't you?" (*FA* 24). She is fed up with the licentiousness of her age. When Henry first makes amorous overtures to her, she, thinking that he is taking undue liberties with her, taking her to be merely a nurse of easy virtue, slaps him hard. Later, she explains that she "couldn't stand the nurse's evening off aspect of it" (*FA* 23). In a chaotic world, she reinstates romance by a kind of ritual of pledging love and fidelity :

> She looked at me, 'And you do love me?'
> 'Yes.'
> 'You did say you loved me, didn't you?'
> 'Yes,' I lied, 'I love you.' I had not said it before.
> 'And you call me Catherine?'

'Catherine,' we walked on a way and were stopped under a tree.

> Say, 'I've come back to Catherine in the night.'
> 'I've come back to Catherine in the night.'
> 'Oh, darling, you have come back, haven't you?'
> 'Yes.'
> 'I love you so, and it's been awful. You won't go away?'
> 'No, I'll always come back.'
> 'Oh, I love you so.' (*FA* 26)

She goes through the ritual, even when she is aware of its unreality :

> 'This is a rotten game we play, isn't it?'
> 'What game?'
> 'Don't be dull.'
> 'I'm not, on purpose.'
> 'You're a nice boy,' she said, 'And you play it as well as you know how.'
> 'But it's a rotten game.' (*FA* 27)

Running away from the present she wants to continue this game of role-playing :

> 'Tell me how many people have you ever loved?'
> 'Nobody.'
> 'Not me even?'
> 'Yes, you.'
> 'How many others really?'
> 'None.'
> 'How many have you — how do you say it? — stayed with?'
> 'None.'
> 'You're lying tome.'
> 'Yes.'
> 'It's all right. Keep right on lying to me. That's what I want you to do.' (*FA* 78)

She re-establishes patriarchy by alleging complete submission : "I'll say just what you wish and I'll do what you wish and then you will never want any other girls, will you?" She looked at me very happily. "I'll do what you want and say what you want and then I'll be a great success, won't I?" "I want what you want. There isn't any me anymore. Just what you want" (*FA* 79).

In the then circumstances, marriages as a sacrament and institution is seen to have become obsolete : "Fight or die. That's what people do. They don't marry" (*FA* 80).

Marriage is looked up as an arrangement of convenience :

> We said to each other that we were married the first day she had come to the hospital and we counted months from our wedding day. I wanted to be really married but Catherine said that if we were they would send her away, and if we merely started on the formalities, they would watch her and would break us up. We would have to be married under Italian law and the formalities were terrific. I wanted us to be married really because I worried about having a child if I thought about it, but we pretended to ourselves we were married and did not worry much and I suppose I enjoyed not being married really. I know one night we talked about it and Catherine said, 'But darling, they'd send me away. What good would it do to marry now? We're really married. I couldn't be any more married.'
>
> 'I only wanted to for you.'
>
> 'There isn't any me. I'm you. Don't make up a separate me.'
>
> 'I thought girls always wanted to be married.'
>
> 'They do. But, darling, I am married. I'm married to you. Don't I make you a good wife?'
>
> 'You see, darling. I had one experience of waiting to be married' (*FA* 84-85).

It is not a religious sacrament for them :

> 'There's no way to be married except by church or state. We are married privately. You see, darling, it would mean everything to me if I had any religion. But I haven't any religion.

Catherine only has faith in Henry and says :

> 'You're my religion.' (*FA* 85)

In the age of Bretts and Daisys, Catherine is faithful :

> 'I'm not unfaithful darling. I've plenty of faults but I'm very faithful, you'll be sick of me I'll be so faithful.' (*FA* 86).

Again, in the circumstances 'a child — a natural outcome of marriage — is seen as a biological trap.' Hemingway offers only one alternative — a private peace :

> 'We won't fight.'
>
> 'We mustn't. Because there's only us two and in the world there's all the rest of them. If anything comes between us we're gone and then they have us." (*FA* 102)

In the time anaesthetized by liquor, Catherine doesn't indulge in hard drinks :

> "Didn't you ever drink brandy?"
>
> "No, darling. I'm a very old fashioned wife." (*FA* 102)

In a rootless society, lacking the security of a home, Catherine and Henry make a home of the room in the hospital and the hotel room. Values and propriety are seen objectively, without the jaundiced view of the Church :

> 'I wish we could do something really sinful,' Catherine said, Everything we do seems so innocent and simple. I can't believe we do anything wrong.' (*FA* 113)

The role of the mate is merged with that of the mother. Slowly she takes over and becomes the matriarch : "You're such a silly boy," she said, "But I'll look after you." (*FA* 180)

Speculating further on marriage and legitimacy, Henry holds legitimacy of the child only a technicality, and marriage a mental state (*FA* 208). As for appearance, long hair is a constant symbol of femininity, in some of Hemingway's novels. Like Romero, Henry expects Catherine to have long hair. He says, "I won't let you cut yours" [your hair], and Catherine, in turn, asks him to grow his beard [a traditional symbol of masculinity] (*FA* 212). Yet, in this regard, there is the new woman's affirmation of will : "You know, darling, I'm not going to cut my hair now until after young Catherine's born. I look too big and matronly now. But after she's born and I'm there again I'm going to cut it and then I'll be a fine new and different girl for you. You won't say I can't, will you?" (*FA* 216)

Catherine emerges a vibrant character who has a strong sense of personal honour, a developed moral sense and a distinct independent and thinking personality, which she retains up to the end. Much against what has been said to the contrary, she is not a dream; rather it is she who slaps the narrator into reality. She is a feminists' ideal — economically independent, assailed by the trauma of war and existentialism, able to see religion in the right perspective, and capable of distinguishing between ritual and true morality, seeking meaning in life and feeling restricted in the limited feminine role. Her body proves to be her trap. She tries to overcome it through modern medicine and surgery but fails. Thus, in the character of Catherine, Hemingway explores a woman's attempt to find private peace in the patriarchal framework through selfless love.

As in his trilogy, Hemingway is also most explicit about the then-current gender roles in his short story "The Snows of Kilimanjaro" (1933). Against the background of his confessional novels *The Sun Also Rises* and *A Farewell to Arms*, the author gives a more objective view of gender roles by taking up the objective omniscient author's stance in the story. Take the case of his characters Helen and Henry. They are of the Parisian stock. Helen is economically independent, extremely efficient, and an avid reader. She hunts, drinks, smokes and leads a life of comradeship with her lover. But there are some undercurrents of dissatisfaction. This apparently new women has a past which wins the reader's sympathy. She suffers from the malaise which Kate Millett later recognizes as the problem that has no name. Her husband dies when she is still a comparatively young woman, and for a while she deviates herself to her grown-up children, who do not need her in any case. To kill her ennui she diverts herself with her home, horses, books and liquor. When all these fail, she takes lovers, but the lovers bore her. She wants a meaningful relation, and starts one with Harry. Harry suffers from the characteristic modern problem of inaction and lassitude.

Helen is a rich woman, and Harry is economically dependent on her. There is an inversion of the traditional roles : the woman is a rich and active bread-winner, the man is a passive recipient of favours. Though he readily accepts and enjoys her wealth, Harry resents her economic dominance. On her part, Helen has submitted herself totally in the true patriarchal spirit : "That's not fair, it was always yours as much as mine. I left everything and I went wherever you wanted to go and I've done what you wanted to do" ("SK" 89).

Helen has made her private peace on Harry's terms, and hence Harry can't find fault with her. Yet, he is irritated and wishes she had stayed with her own people, and not meddled with his life. From her side, her relationship with Harry is a quest for meaning in life, but on Harry's part, it is a bargain. Looking into the relationship, Harry as Hemingway's spokesman has to admit that it is the man who has relinquished his dominant role and not the woman who has usurped it. He feels that women feels feminist compulsion of assertion only when their male counterparts lack vigour, vitality and virility. The women's emasculation is triggered by men who are effeminate. Harry has an epiphanic realisation : "It was not her fault that when he went to her he was already over and when he went to her he spoke only from habit and in order to be comfortable" ("SK" 93). He further admits :

> He had destroyed his talent himself. Why should he blame this woman, because she kept him well? He had destroyed his talent by not using it, by betrayals of himself and what he believed in. By drinking so much that he blunted the edge of his perceptions, by laziness, by sloth and by snobbery, by pride and by prejudice, by hook and crook. What was his talent anyway? It was a talent all right, but instead of using it he had traded on it. It was never what he had done but always what he could do. And he had chosen to make his living with something else instead of a pen or a pencil. It was strange, too, that when he fell in love with another woman she should always have more money than the last one ("SK" 94).

Helen has suffered a lot and is now really broken. She pleads : "I'm only a middle-aged woman who loves you and wants to do what you want to do. I've been destroyed two or three times already" ("SK" 97). About their relationship, Harry has to admit that she has been very good to him and it is he who has been cruel and unjust to her : "She was a fine woman, marvelous really" ("SK" 97). He blames his own passivity. In the past, his relationships with women were full-blooded ones, in which he loved too much, demanded too much and wore himself out, contrasted with the business-like arrangement he has with Helen. Writing retrospectively in 1943, Hemingway admits as much : "Take as good a woman as Pauline — a hell of a wonderful woman and once she turns mean, although, of course, it is your own actions that turn her mean — mine I mean..." (Baker *SL* 554). In the present circumstances, when men fight and die or break down, the blame falls on women, so that, women have not only to bear the trauma of the failure of the social order but are also held largely responsible for it. What's more, they are required to carry out the social struggle as if nothing has happened. In an age of anxiety, it is women who are required to offer an alternative.

The last of the trilogy, *For Whom the Bell Tolls*, is a treatise on the complementary nature of the genders. The whole action takes place on a spiritual plane. The main female characters of the novel, Maria is dismissed as more of a dream than a woman. Criticising her for her lack of independent identity, Edmund Wilson calls her the amoebae-like Spanish girl Maria. Maria and Pilar (the other woman character) are, in fact, one character broken into two. As the action takes place in a very short span of time, the one is the other's past, that is one doesn't have to stretch the imagination too far to imagine that Pilar too must have been as innocent as Maria in her youth. Similarly by speculating into Maria's future one can foresee that with the passage of time she will become as hard as Pilar. In Maria, Hemingway works out the Lily Virgin archetype, and portrays her as very vulnerable and naïve, in spite of what she has suffered. She is the daughter of the mayor, and hence, the target of the revolutionaries. She has been at Valladolid, the centre of the revolutionary activity, where her head was shaved. But, when the book opens, she has recovered from the trauma to the extent that she jokes about her shaven hair : "That is the way I comb it," she said to Robert Jordan and laughed" (*WBT* 25). Contrasted with her is Pilar, who stands apart by virtue to her strength and fortitude — she is compared to granite : A woman of about fifty, almost as big as Pablo, almost as wide as she is tall, in black peasant shirt and black heavy wool socks on heavy legs, black rope-soled shoes and with a brown face like a model for a granite monument. She has big but nice-looking hands, and her thick curly hair is twisted into a knot on her neck (*WBT* 32-33).

Pilar takes charge of the leadership of the group after Pablo's breakdown. Pablo was once very efficient and widely acclaimed but is now only a wreck. She admits to Robert Jordan : "He was a very good man, but now he is terminated" (*WBT* 34). Other characters confirm her view that "Pablo himself was brave in the beginning" and "killed more people than cholera" (*WBT* 28). But, now is a broken man who drinks too much and wants to retire like a matador de toros. In the circumstances Pilar perforce has to take over. But once she has taken over, she is determined to be an efficient matriarch of the group. She looks after the interests of the people in the camp. It is Pilar who makes the others of her group carry Maria when she passes out during the train explosion. After she takes Maria under her wing she takes good care of her and creates a good rapport with her : "How does she get along with the girl, Maria?" Robert Jordan asked. "Good. She likes the girl" (*WBT* 30). She looks for masculine energy and disapproves of Pablo's drinking habits and emasculation. In contrast, she approves of Jordan, who emanates masculine strength : "You're bigger than you look," and runs her hand over his shoulder, feeling the muscle under the flannel shirt (*WBT* 34).

As a matriarch caring for Maria like a daughter she warns Jordan before entrusting her to him : "Be very good and careful about the girl...she has had a bad time, understandest thou ?" (*WBT* 34). Pilar is invested with the Earth Mother — the mystic woman — archetype. She sees Jordan's hand and can foresee doom in it. There is a steady transfer of roles, so that like a true mother Pilar initiates Maria into the role of a wife :

> 'I must go to Pilar. She is giving me instruction.'
>
> 'What does she give thee?'
>
> 'Instruction.' She smiled at him and then kissed him. 'Did you never hear of religious instruction?' She blushed. 'It is something like that,' she blushed again, 'But different.' (*WBT* 329)

Maria accepts the feminine role completely, including that of taking good care of her man :

> 'I will buy a clean wedding shirt for thee. Dost ever wash thy shirt?'
>
> 'Sometimes.'
>
> 'I will keep everything clean and I will pour thy whisky and put water in it as it was done at Sordo's.' (*WBT* 324)

Marriage as a religious ceremony has lost its meaning in the contemporary world, which is sans faith : "If you wish," she said. "But since we no longer have the Church I do not think it carries importance" (*WBT* 324).

But marriage as a physical, social and spiritual bonding is still looked forward to. The authorial comment highlighting the physical aspect of the union is : "He felt the earth move out and away from under them" (*WBT* 154). This comment has evoked much critical laughter. For the matrimonial bond to be meaningful, it is important that it should be based on total honesty, and Maria confides in great detail to Jordan about her having been gang-raped, shaving of her head, and her fear that she might not be able to bear a child. She is very much aware of risk of rejection by him.

In the denouement of the novel, marriage is discussed further. It is looked on as a spiritual union of individuals, a union in which social and religious sanction is irrelevant :

> 'We are married now. I marry thee now. Thou art my wife. But go to sleep, my rabbit, for there is little time now….' 'Good night, my husband.' 'Good night,' he said, 'Good night, wife.' (*WBT* 334)

Jordan finds Maria to be a true companion, one in whom all feminine roles are merged :

> Maria is my true love and my wife. I never had a true love. I never had a wife. She is also my sister, and I never had a sister, and my daughter and I never will have a daughter. (*WBT* 358)

The union sought in marriage becomes all the more perfect when it is purely spiritual. At the end of the novel, Robert Jordan's and Maria's distinct identities merge into one composite whole. Jordan puts it thus : "I go always with thee wherever thou goest" (*WBT* 434). And he says elsewhere : "Thou wilt go now, rabbit. But I go with thee. As long as there is one of us there is both of us" (*WBT* 435). Jordan distinguishes between a mortal being and a spiritual one. As a mortal being everyone is alone and has to face death too alone : "that [facing death] people cannot do together. Each one must do it alone" (*WBT* 435). But on the spiritual plane an intermingling of identities is possible : "There is no good-bye, because we are not apart" (*WBT* 436).

Thus, for Hemingway, between men and women, personalities different, distinct and one exclusive of the other are less than ideal. To him, each is a part of a complete whole, and one is incomplete without the other. Says the epigraph of the novel :

> No man is an Island, intire of itself, every man is a piece of the continent, a part of the maine; if a clod bee washed away by the Sea, Europe is the lesse, as well as if a Promonotorie were; any man's death diminishes mee, because I am involved in Mankinde. And therefore never send to know for whom the bell tolls; it tolls for thee. (John Donne)

Thus, Hemingway reaffirms his faith in feminine strength.

From the above discussion it is seen that Hemingway recognizes a marked change having taken place during the feminist movement, in the feminine psyche, and the fact that the change, good or bad, is irrevocable. (Brett cannot grow her hair; Catherine cannot have a home and a child; Maria has to come to terms with life's uncertainty.) Freud has a deep impact on the western thought and psyche. Female sexuality and liberation are new and hot topics of discussion in Hemingway's time. As a reaction to Freud, esteem for the female sex is at an all-time low, and Hemingway's contemporaries have misogynist views. F. Scott. Fitzgerald in *The Great Gatsby* (1925), Richard Aldington in *The Death of a Hero* (1929), T.S. Eliot in "The Wasteland" and D.H. Lawrence in his poems and stories written towards the close of his life were all bitter towards women. Lawrence held the then widely held view that there was destruction implicit in all female ambition. As against this, in his novels, Hemingway seems to generally maintain a rather sympathetic attitude to the female aspiration, and yet he would not hold twainness or opposition between man and woman necessary or worthwhile. Brett does not like to be "A bitch who ruins children"; Catherine submits completely to Henry's wishes; Maria has no separate self from Jordan's; and Helen would always do what Harry wants her to, and for all these heroines of his, Hemingway seems to have immense sympathy. In fact, it is men who are targets of his bitter invective. Harry of "Snows of Kilmanjaro" seems to wonder why the men of his generation should blame women for their emasculation, for it is they themselves who are responsible for it. Thus, Hemingway holds a positive view about the feminist turn of events, and, in fact, through his novels, tries to give the women's aspiration a healthy direction.

Hemingway holds man and woman not as opposites, but as complementary to each other. Moveover, in all his works considered above, he holds that it is women who can provide an alternative to the present humdrum state of affairs. In *The Sun Also Rises*, it is Brett's decision to put a stop to sexual anarchy. In *A Farewell to Arms*, it is Catherine who once again affirms faith in life's possibilities for warmth and affection, and in *For Whom the Bell Tolls*, it is Maria and Pilar who are entrusted with continuing the struggle of a society in flux. Again, in "Snows of Kilimanjaro," it is Helene who must seek answers to some of the existentialist questions. Hence, the picture that emerges of the Hemingway woman is that of one who is faced with the same existentialist questions as men, and of one who bids fair to survive the trauma involved better than men. In any case, it is not possible to agree with the opinion of Baker that "Hemingway shares with many of his predecessors an outlook undoubtedly masculine, a certain chivalric attitude, not without ironic overtone, and a distinction to interest himself in what may be called the prosaisms of the female world."

Indeed, in a sense *The Sun Also Rises*, *A Farewell to Arms*, *For Whom the Bell Tolls* and "Snows of Kilimanjaro" are virtual case histories of women. It is the women's fate which is the centre of attention, and it is their heroic stance, their moment of epiphany, which is the denouement of each of these works. Though Hemingway nowhere commits himself in so many words on the question of emancipation of women, the very fact that he does not assign them to a separate limited sphere but rather makes them participants in the same questions with which men are engaged regarding the meaning of life, such as sexual liberty and war, speaks volumes for his support to the women's cause. He puts women on a plane where they duly share with men the quest of the human spirit for the meaning of life, where, in fact, the gender difference cease to exist.

## WORK CITED

Aldridge, John W., *After the Lost Generation : A Critical Study of the Writers of Two Wars*. New York : McGraw-Hill, 1951.

Baker, Carlos, *Ernest Hemingway : A Life Story*. New York : Charles Scribner's Sons, 1969.

——, *Ernest Hemingway : Selected Letters, 1917-1961*. New York : Charles Scribner's Sons, 1981.

Baker, Sheridan, *Ernest Hemingway : An Introduction and Interpretation*. New York : Holt, Rinehart and Winston, 1976.

Bardacke, Theodore, "Hemingway's Women". Ernest Hemingway : *The Man and This Work*. Ed. John K.M. McCaffery. New York : World, 1950.

Benson, Jackson J., *Hemingway : The Writer's Art of Self-Defense*. Minneapolis : University of Minnesota, 1969.

Bernice, Kert, *The Hemingway Women*. New York : Norton, 1983.

Bradbury, Malcolm and David Palmer, eds., *The American Novel and The Nineteen-Twenties*. London: Edward Arnold, 1971.

Brenner, Gerry, *Concealments in Hemingway's Works*. Columbus : Ohio State UP, 1983.

Brooks, Cleanth, *The Hidden God : Studies in Hemingway, Faulkner, Yeats, Eliot and Warren*. New Haven, Connecticut : Yale UP, 1963.

Brown, Dorothy M., *Setting a Course : American Women in the 1920s*. Boston : Twayne, 1987.

Bruccoli, Mathew, ed., *Ernest Hemingway*. Facsimile Edition. 2 vols. Detroit : Omnigraphics, 1990.

Burnam, Tom, "Primitivism and Masculinity in the Works of Ernest Hemingway." *Modern Fiction Studies* 1.3 (August 1955) : 21.

Cooperman, Stanley, *World War I and the American Novel*. Baltimore : The John Hopkins, 1947, 185.

Cowley, Malcolm, Introduction. *Hemingway. Viking Portable Library* ed. New York : Viking Press, 1944, rpt. As "Nightmare and Ritual in Hemingway." *Hemingway : A Collection of Critical Essays*. Ed. Robert P. Weeks. Englewood Cliffs, N.J. : Prentice-Hall, 1962, 40-51.

Dahiya, Bhim S., *The Hero in Hemingway : A Study in Development*. Chandigarh : Bahri Publications Ltd., 1978.

Donaldson, Scott, *By Force of Will : The Life and Art of Ernest Hemingway*. New York : Viking, 1977.

Duffey, Bernard J., ed., *Modern American Literature*. New York and Chicago : Holt, Rinehart and Winston, 1964.

Eastman, Max, "Bull in the Afternoon." *New Republic* 75 (June 1933) : 94-97.

Fenton, Charles A., *The Apprenticeship of Ernest Hemingway : The Early Years*. New York : Farrar, Straus and Young, 1954.

Fleishman, Fritz, *American Novelists Revisited : Essays in Feminist Criticism*. Boston : Ohio State UP, 1983.

Geismar, Maxwell, "Ernest Hemingway : You Could Always Come Back." *Writers in Crisis : The American Novel Between Two Wars*. Boston : Houghton, Mifflin, 1942, 39-85.

Grant, Naomi M., "The Role of Woman in the Fiction of Ernest Hemingway." *Dissertation Abstracts* 29 : 4456A.

Grebstein, Sheldon N., *Hemingway's Craft*. Carbondale : South Illinois UP, 1973.

Hatchett, F., "*Hemingway : A Farewell to Arms.*" *Saturday Review of Literature* 32 (6 Aug. 1949) : 32-33.

Hemingway, Ernest, *The Sun Also Rises*. New York : Charles Scriber's Sons, 1926. Cited as *SAR*.

——, *A Farewell to Arms*. New York : Charles Scribner's Sons, 137. Cited as *FA*.

——, *For Whom the Bell Tolls*. New York : Charles Scriber's Sons, 1940. Cited as *WBT*.

Hemingway, Leicester, *My Brother, Ernest Hemingway*. Cleveland : World, 1961.

Hemingway, Marcelline Sanford, *At The Hemingway's : A Family Portrait*. Boston : Little, Brown, 1962.

Hotchner, A.E., *Papa Hemingway*. New York : Random House, 1966.

Kashkeen, Ivan, "Ernest Hemingway : A Tragedy of Craftsmanship." *International Literature* 5 (1935).

Killinger, John, *Hemingway and The Dead Gods : A Study in Existentialism*. Lexington : U of Kentucky Press, 1961.

Larson, Kelli A., *Ernest Hemingway : A Reference Guide* (1974-1989). Boston : G.K. Hall, 1990.

Lewis, Robert William, *Hemingway on Love*. Austin : U of Texas Press, 1965.

Lynn, Kenneth S., *Hemingway*. New York : Simon and Schuster, 1987.

Machlin, Milt, *The Private Hell of Ernest Hemingway*. New York : Paperback Library, 1962.

Martin, Wendy, "Brett Ashley as New Woman." *New Essays on The Sun Also Rises*. Ed. Linda Wagner Martin. CUP, 1987, 65-82.

Miller, Linda Patterson, "Hemingway's Women : A Re-assessment." "*Hemingway in Italy*" *and Other Essays*. Ed. Robert W. Lewis. New York : Praeger, 1990.

Nahal, Chaman, *The Narrative Pattern in Ernest Hemingway's Fiction*. Delhi : Vikas Publications, 1971.

Nolan, Charles J., "Hemingway's Women's Movement." *The Hemingway Review* 3.2 (Spring 1984).

Peterson, Richard, *Hemingway : Direct and Oblique*. The Hague and Paris : Mouton, 1969.

Raeburn, John, *Fame Became Him : Hemingway as Public Writer*. Bloomington : Indian U Press, 1984.

Reynolds, Michael, *The Young Hemingway*. Oxford : Basil Blackwell, 1986.

——, S., *Hemingway's First War : The Making of A Farewell to Arms*. Princeton UP, 1976.

Rovit, Earl, *Ernest Hemingway*. New York : Twayne, 1963.

Schneider, Dorothy and Carl J. Schneider, *American Women in the Progressive Era, 1900-1920*. New York : Facts of File, 1993.

Scholes, Robert and Nancy R. Comley, *Hemingway's Genders : Rereading the Hemingway Text*. New Haven : YUP, 1994.

Schwartz, Delmore, "Ernest Hemingway's Literary Situation," *Southern Review*. 3 (1939) : 769-82.

Singer, Kurt D., *Hemingway : Life and Death of a Giant*. Los Angeles : Holloway House, 1962.

Smiley, Pamela, "Gender-Linked Miscommunication in *Hills Like White Elephants*." *The Hemingway Review* 3.2 (Spring 1984).

Smith, Carol H., "Women and the Loss of Eden in Hemingway's Mythology." *Ernest Hemingway : The Writer in Context*. Ed. James Nagel. Madison : U of Wiscosin P, 1984.

Spanier, Sandra, "Catherine Barkley and the Hemingway Code : Ritual and Survival in *A Farewell to Arms*" in *Ernest Hemingway's A Farewell to Arms* ed. Harold Bloom, New York : Chelsea House, 1986.

Spilka, Mark, *Hemingway's Quarrel with Androgyny*. Lincoln and London : U of Nebraska Press, 1990.

Svoboda, Frederick J., *Hemingway and The Sun Also Rises*. Lawrence : U Press of Kansas, 1983.

Wagner, Linda W., "Proud and Friendly and Gently : Women in Hemingway's Early Fiction." *Ernest Hemingway : The Papers of a Writer*. Ed. Bernard Oldsey. New York : Garland, 1981, 63-71.

——, *Hemingway and Faulkner : Inventors / Masters*. Methuen, New Jersey : The Scarecrow Press, 1975.

Waldhorn, Arthur, *A Reader's Guide to Ernest Hemingway*. New York : Farrar, Straus and Giroux, 1973.

Watkins, Floyd C., *The Flesh and the Word : Eliot, Hemingway, Faulkner*. Nashville : Wanderbilt U Press, 1971.

Weeks, Robert P., *Hemingway : A Collection of Critical Essays*, Twentieth Century Views. Englewood Cliffs, N.J. : Prentice-Hall, Inc., 1962.

Wexler, Joyce, "E.R.A. For Hemingway : A Feminist Defense of *A Farewell to Arms*." Georgia Review 35.1 (1981) : 111-23.

Wilson, Edmund, "Hemingway : Gauge of Morale." *The Wound and the Bow : Seven Studies in Literature*. London U. Paperbacks. London : UP, 1941.

Wylder, Delbert E., *Hemingway's Heroes*. Alburquerque : U of New Mexico P, 1969.

Young, Philip, *Ernest Hemingway*. New York : Rinehart and Co., Inc., 1952.

——, *Ernest Hemingway : A Reconsideration*. University Park and London : Pennsylvania State UP, 1966, 70.

# 7

# Theme of *Nada* in Ernest Hemingway's Major Novels

*—Mary Mohanty*

ERNEST HEMINGWAY prefaces his first novel, *The Sun Also Rises* (1926), with an epigraph from *Ecclesiastes*, emphasising the transience of life and all human efforts against the eternal nature :

> "One generation passeth away, and another generation cometh : but the earth abideth forever..." (*Ecclesiastes* 1 : 4).

This theme is central to all of Hemingway's works. In all his works he has depicted the theme of life's futility and the ineffectuality of all human endeavour against the background of an eternal nature. The futility of man's efforts appears all the more intensely against the backdrop of the everlasting earth. This sense of despair and the recognition of this futile effort of man is called by Hemingway Nada, a Spanish word which means "nothing" or "nothingness."

As a result Hemingway's world is a violent world not congenial for human living. It is a world of violence, death or war. This violence, death, destruction and war symbolise Hemingway's sense of *Nada* that annihilates human aspirations and life. Hemingway states this through the protagonist Frederic Henry in *A Farewell to Arms* :

> If people bring so much courage to this world the world has to kill them to break them, so of course it kills them. The world breaks everyone and afterward many are

> strong at the broken places. But those that will not break it kills. It kills the very good and the very gentle and the very brave impartially. If you are none of these you can be sure it will kill you too but there will be no special hurry (249).

So the world impartially kills the brave, the good and the gentle and those who are none of these. Only the time of killing may differ from person to person, nonetheless it kills everybody. More important in this connection is the fact that even a courageous person is not exempt from this "killing." The world of Ernest Hemingway is a world of all pervasive gloom. The breaking of the man is symbolized by the "wound." The would may be either physical or psychological or both. This "wound" renders man a physical and emotional cripple, that is, it causes emotional tension in man and, sometimes, renders him a physical and emotional cripple.

Looking back down the corridors and Hemingway's life this sense of gloom or *Nada* can be traced to his traumatic experience in the trench — mortar shell explosion on the Italian Front in 1918 during the first World War. Ernest Hemingway was a member of the voluntary ambulance corps on the Italian Front when he was wounded. The traumatic neurosis that followed was not only physical, but psychic as well. The undeserved would broke his relation with the past, with the society and anything ideal. He was again and again haunted by that experience which shattered his emotional being forcing Hemingway to be an expatriate writer.

So the wound recurs in all of his fictions. The protagonist is wounded in all the fictions either physically or psychically or both. While the first protagonist Nick Adams in, *In Our Time* is wounded in the knee, Jake Barnes in *The Sun Also Rises* is emasculated by war, Frederic Henry in *A Farewell to Arms* is again wounded in the knee at the Italian Front in the First World War, Harry Morgan loses his arm in *To Have and Have Not*, Robert Jordan's leg is crushed in *For Whom the Bell Tolls*, Colonel Cantwell has his cardiac trouble and bad hand in *Across the River and into the Trees*, and finally the wounds of Santiago are clearly seen in *The Old Man and the Sea*.

The background of all of Ernest Hemingway's fictions are either war or war-like conditions that symbolize the ruthlessness, cruelty and brutality of the outside world and in which all human effort is rendered fruitless. In *The Sun Also Rises* the background is not immediate war as in *A Farewell to Arms* or *For Whom the Bell Tolls*. But it is the after-effect of war which is equally frightening. In *A Farewell to Arms* the action takes place in the midst of war as in *For Whom the Bell Tolls*. In both these fictions the worlds is full of perils, horror, violence, tension and apprehension. In *To Have and Have Not* the entire atmosphere is tense with bitter conflict. In *Across the River and into the Trees* though the physical war is over, the tension continues. In *The Old Man and the Sea* the old man Santiago fights an elemental battle against the hostile forces in the Gulf Stream. The Gulf Stream, so long symbolically expressed in earlier fictions, comes to the forefront.

Though Ernest Hemingway depicts darkness and death as the manifestations of *Nada* in his fictions, it is not a world of unrelieved gloom. Hemingway holds out some hope for the broken and wounded human beings. There is a ray of sunshine amidst the encircling gloom of this world. He underscores certain qualities that a man must possess in order to survive or win the battle against the hostile forces of the world. These qualities are called "code of conduct." These qualities are love, courage, endurance, self-respect, pride, honour, honesty and integrity. Ernest Hemingway was obsessed with violence and death by his traumatic experience in the Italian Front. So he went to Spain in order to see life and death in the Spanish bull rings. In *Death in the Afternoon* he says :

> The only place where you could see life and death, *i.e.*, violent death now that the wars were over, was in the bull ring and I wanted very much to go to Spain where I could study it. I was trying to learn to write, commencing with the simplest things, and one of the simplest things of all

> and the most fundamental is violent death. It has none of the complications of death by disease, or so-called natural death, or the death of a friend or someone you have loved or have hated, but it is death nevertheless, one of the subjects that a man may write of (10).

There in the bull ring Ernest Hemingway found the microcosm of man pitted against the outside hostile forces symbolized in the matador facing the bull. A matador faces death in the form of bulls in the bull ring. A matador must follow a certain code of conduct in order to kill the bull with honour and dignity. And there lies his honesty and integrity as a true bullfighter. Hemingway says in *Death in the Afternoon* that bull-fighting is the only art in which "the degree of brilliance in the performance is left to the fighter's honour. In Spain honour is a very real thing. Called *pundonor*, it means honour, probity, courage, self-respect, and pride in one word" (90). In other words the matador must have courage to endure or suffer or face death without complaint, but with honour, self-respect and dignity. Hemingway further adds in the same context, that honour, courage, and glory are not abstract values for the Spaniards. They "may be as real a thing as water, wine or olive oil" (p. 91). The Spaniards' or matador's pride is central to his attitude to death and killing as Hemingway puts it in *Death in the Afternoon* :

> Once you accept the rule of death thou shalt not kill is an easily and a naturally obeyed commandment. But when a man is still in rebellion against death he has pleasure in taking to himself one of the Godlike attributes — that of giving it. This is one of the most profound feelings in those men who enjoy killing. These things are done in pride, and pride, of course, is a Christian sin, and a pagan virtue. But it is pride which makes the bullfight and a true enjoyment of killing which makes the great matador (221).

The matador's pride enables him to go on fighting, trying to "kill" the bull with love and honesty and integrity, though he may not succeed. His victory lies in fighting the good fight to the best of his capacity irrespective of the result. Hemingway says in *Death in the Afternoon* :

> "A bullfighter is not always expected to be good, only to do his best" (90).

So this struggle of the matador confers moral victory on him though he may fail in the material plane. Following the great matadors like Villaita, Joselito, Juan Belmote, Manuel Garcia and many others Ernest Hemingway finds in their qualities a means to overcome death and darkness, that is *Nada*. These qualities provide a "clean well-lighted place", the *Nada* conscious old waiter does not leave the well-lighted cafe which provides temporary shelter against *Nada*. These qualities constitute "grace under pressure."

In Hemingway's fictions the protagonists are afraid of darkness and they cannot sleep without light. Darkness manifests *Nada* in their hearts. Love constitutes the main source for sustaining life amidst *Nada* and hence Hemingway repeatedly portrays love amidst the brutality and ruthlessness of war; and it is often crushed by war. He also depicts various stages of love from mere sensual gratification to sublime love or love in the highest sense as defined by the Priest in *A Farewell to Arms* :

> "When you love, you wish to do things for. You wish to sacrifice for. You wish to serve" (72).

In the highest form of love it becomes compassion when man looks upon the world with deeper understanding and greater knowledge fully aware of life's tragic poignancy without any disillusionment.

The theme of *Nada* is prevalent in all the major works of Ernest Hemingway. In *The Sun Also Rises* there is no horror of immediate war. The war is already over. But the characters suffer the sad effects of war. The protagonist Jake Barnes is emasculated by a wound in the war. He is rendered impotent. Jake symbolizes the futility, aimlessness and sterility of the entire post-war generation. Gertrude Stein rightly remarks, "You are all a lost generation." Not only Jake is "lost" physically and emotionally, but the entire generation is "lost." They are psychically wounded. So they lead a gloomy life whiling away their time in drinking and merry-making in cafes in Paris and in Madrid and in sexual promiscuity in order to forget their sad predicament. Jake, symbolizing the lost generation, takes to reporting in order to make a living. His wound has rendered him ineffectual and impotent and hence Jake cannot sleep with lights off. He says that for six months he never slept with the light off. He cannot face the darkness of night which resembles *Nada* and hence is troubled at night, leaves Brett alone in his sitting room and lies down, having "a bad time". Occasionally he makes a fishing trip to Burguete or visits a fiesta at Pamplona which have a therapeutic effect on him.

The futility of life is more vividly expressed in the absence of love in this fiction. Love is not possible among the "wounded" characters. The only love possible is between Jake and Brett. But that is again rendered ineffectual by Jake's emasculation. Besides Brett is a nymphomaniac who seeks pleasures of love in others' arms when love is not possible between her and Jake. But looking at her past she appears helpless as her first love was crushed in the war. Her second love for Jake is also vanquished by war.

However in the midst of post-war gloom hope shines in the form of a code of conduct. The perfect code hero is the matador Romero. He has his honesty and integrity of character. Jake follows the code of conduct to meet the unbearable agonies of life. He suffers pain and tension without any complaint. Brett, in spite of her loose character, upholds honour and integrity when she leaves the matador Pedro Romero and feels rather good about it. She says to Jake :

> "You know it makes one feel rather good deciding not to be a bitch" (245).

At the end of the novel when Jake and Brett are caught in the traffic they realize the need for self-control and self-discipline in order to enjoy what is there in store for them is life. Thus they fight off *Nada* or sense of futility of life with their courage and discipline like a good matador.

In *A Farewell to Arms* the action takes place in the midst of war. Here love is portrayed in the ruthless and brutal arms of war. The atmosphere is tense with all the hurly-burly, tension, murder, and brutality of war. The emotion evoked is one of futility, despair and betrayal. The protagonist Frederic Henry expresses his disbelief of the abstract values. He realizes that abstract words like "honour" and "glory" are meaningless besides the concrete names of rivers, villages, and dates :

> "Abstract words such as glory, honour, courage, or hallow were obscene beside the concrete names of villages, the numbers of roads, the names of rivers, the numbers of regiments, and the dates" (185).

Frederic Henry is wounded like Hemingway in a trench-mortar shell explosion on the Italian Front in the First World War. He is taken for treatment to the military hospital at Milan where he is united in sexual love with the English nurse, Catherine Barkley whom he loves deeply. He cannot sleep and drinks too much in secret. Like all wounded heroes of Hemingway Frederic is haunted by the memory of his wound. Unlike *The Sun Also Rises* where Jake and Brett cannot enjoy sexual love because of Jake's emasculation, here Frederic Henry and Catherine Barkley are free to indulge in love-making. After recuperation Frederic returns to war. But in the Caporetto retreat where the officers are indiscriminately shot he jumps into the river Tagliamento and flees from war, his disillusionment being complete :

> "Anger was washed away in the river along with any obligation.... I was through" (232).

Frederic Henry flees from war and from any obligation to society and tries to make a "separate peace" in the loving arms of Catherine. This is true love and not mere sensual enjoyment to pass off time. Catherine feels as if she were married without the rituals of marriage and both Henry and Catherine flee to the idyllic mountains of Switzerland to escape the horror and brutality of the hostile world. But there in their Eden-like sanctuary which seems to provide a "clean well-lighted place" in the gloom or *Nada* or society, Catherine dies at child birth.

Frederic Henry desperately prays to God for the life of Catherine, but in vain. At the end he is once again left alone with a great shock. The lovers cannot escape the arms of fate and the struggle of life and they fail in their futile attempt to do so. The feeling of betrayal and the closing of a trap is all pervasive in the novel. But the Frederic Henry who flees the arms of war to the arms of love is somehow different from the man who has to bid farewell to the arms of love as well. When Catherine dies at child birth he assures her that he is no afraid; it is only a 'dirty trick" of the fate :

> "I'm not a bit afraid. It's just a dirty trick" (331).

When he returns to the Swiss hotel in the rain after Catherine's death, he is a stronger man with a better understanding of life. The all pervading gloom, despair and sense of *Nada* seem to offer little hope. It breaks Henry partially and Catherine fully. The love of Frederic and Catherine provide only temporary relief in the engulfing *Nada*.

In his major novel of love and war *For Whom the Bell Tolls* Ernest Hemingway interweaves the theme of *Nada*, the fight between the essence of life-love and nothingness, war and destruction into the historic event of the Spanish Civil War. The Spanish Civil War is not only a war between the Spanish Loyalists and the foreign-aided Fascists of Franco, but symbolically it is a war between life and death, or good and evil, or light and darkness. In the novel the protagonist Robert Jordan, an American teaching Spanish in the University of Montana, voluntarily joins the Loyalist guerrillas in Guadarrama mountains as a dynamiter. He feels that he fights not only for the Republican cause, but for the cause of humanity as well. He fights for liberty, equality and fraternity or, in other words, for life and its values which are threatened by Fascism. The Fascist bombers symbolize the forces of evil that annihilate life and hence they represent symbolically *Nada*. The high mountain sanctuary of Sierra de Guadarramas is like a clean well-lighted place. The guerrillas live here in primitive conditions protected from the fear of annihilation by Fascism. Here the weather is soothing, calm and clear and Hemingway creates a kind of idyll in the midst of war. It is in this Eden-like place that Maria, raped and ruined by the Falangists, is restored to life and sanity by the true love of Jordan. The idyllic forest provides a sanctuary for true love-making of the lovers, Jordan and Maria, in the midst of war. However the "clean well-lighted place" of the mountains is not a permanent refuge against *Nada*. El Sordo's guerrilla band is destroyed on the hill-top by aerial bombardment by three Fascist planes. Similarly, when the bridge is blown, Pablo's mountain cave can no longer provide shelter against annihilation. It becomes vulnerable to attack. So Pablo and his group escape to the Sierra de Gredos in another mountain. But the fear of attack is not totally ruled out.

But Ernest Hemingway depicts true love between Robert Jordan and Maria, and the defiant and courageous fight of Robert Jordan as two images of "a clean well-lighted place." They confer victory on the protagonist in spite of the fact that the lovers are separated for ever and Jordan precariously holds life with his badly crushed leg at the end. Here Hemingway depicts the sublime love as defined by the Priest in *A Farewell to Arms*. In *For Whom the Bell Tolls* Robert Jordan, a foreigner, truly loves the raped girl Maria. Having hardly three days for love-making they reach the intensity and poignancy of the highest kind of love. There is complete merger of body and soul in the lovers. Like Catherine, Robert Jordan says that they are already married without the fake rituals. He consoles Maria,

> "We are married, now. I marry thee now.
> Thou art my wife."

And again : "I am thee and thou art me and all of one is the other" (235-51).

It is the love that gives meaning to life in the foreboding gloom of annihilation. And Robert Jordan recognises the value of their love :

> "But I tell you it is true and that you have it and that you are lucky even if you die tomorrow" (289).

At the end Robert Jordan compels Maria to escape with the band of Pablo with the most moving words and, most important, emphasizing their union of souls;

> "As long as there is one of us there is both of us."
> "The me in thee. Now you go for us both. Truly. We both go in thee now" (437).

Beside Jordan-Maria relationship, Jordan's courageous and defiant fight against the fascists provides him victory in the spiritual plane. Robert Jordan displays courage, pride, endurance and dignity at the moment of truth and thereby he wins over death by symbolically slaying death on the spiritual plane. His physical death is nullified by his spiritual victory over death. In the last chapter Robert Jordan is left alone with his wounded leg when Pablo's band escapes to Sierra de Gredos with his beloved Maria. It is his pride and courage that enable him to persuade Maria to go with Pablo's band. No doubt Jordan suffers the pangs of separation and the severe pain of the wounded leg; but he endures the suffering with courage. His sense of fortitude enables him to hold on when the pain is unbearable. "I will take whatever I get", he says (442). Though the memory of his father's suicide comes to his mind again and again, he resists the temptation with the determination to check the Fascist approach in order to cover the guerrilla band's escape. Hemingway beautifully describes his defiant posture at the end :

> "Robert Jordan lay behind the tree holding onto himself very carefully and delicately to keep his hands steady" (444).

In his masterpiece *The Old Man and the Sea*, which won Hemingway the Pulitzer prize in 1952 and the Noble Prize in 1954, Hemingway treats the theme of *Nada* in a more explicit manner. Here the struggle between man versus nature is obvious in the setting of the fiction. In this novel Hemingway makes the Gulf Stream itself the setting. The Gulf Stream with its giant Marlin and sharks symbolize the hostile forces of nature. The old Cuban fisherman Santiago symbolizes the human race. Santiago alone fights an indefatigable battle against the hostile forces of nature. The Cuban fisherman voyages into the high seas in the Gulf Stream with the hope of catching a large fish after eighty-four days of unsuccessful fishing. He sails alone in a boat far out in the sea where there is no human being to lend a helping hand at the time of need. The very fact that Santiago is all alone in the Gulf Stream signifies the lonely struggle every man has to fight against the dark, hostile force, *viz. Nada* in his own psyche, represented in this novel by the sharks. Though he harpoons a big Marlin, he does not know what is it, and the Marlin drags the old man in another direction. Then there ensues a long struggle between Santiago and the Marlin. After Santiago kills the Marlin he ties it to his boat and sets sail homeward. But on the way he has to fight with the sharks who take away most of the flesh from the Marlin. When Santiago returns to the shore, what he brings home is the skeleton of the giant Marlin. Though Santiago is defeated, his labour lost and his struggle proved futile on the material plane, he wins a moral victory.

Santiago is the best code hero of Ernest Hemingway. He embodies all the qualities of a good matador; courage, endurance, honesty, integrity, good fight and above all love. In the process of fighting against the Marlin and the sharks Santiago is wounded in his hands and head. But he is never worried. He takes his suffering as it comes :

> "He settled comfortably against the wood and took his suffering as it came..." (*EH* 720).

Santiago is defiant and possesses an undefeated heart. His heroism is clear in what he says :

> " 'But man in not made for defeat', he said.
> 'A man can be destroyed but not defeated' " (*EH* 740).

The old man is not only courageous, defiant and endures his pain, he also has the highest kind of love that encompasses anybody and everybody. He is never angry when others make fun of him, and he loves the Marlin as his brother. He is almost sad that he has killed his brother :

> "I am a tired old man. But I have killed this fish which is my brother and now I must do the slave work" (*EH* 736).

Besides Santiago loves the small birds and fishes of the sea. He has love and compassion for them. When he fights with the sharks he fights in self-defence.

In addition to the above Hemingway has depicted Santiago as an old man who has transcended the urge for sexual gratification. So he depicts a higher kind of love, that is compassion. It comes out of a superior knowledge and a better understanding of life.

So at the end Santiago wins a moral victory fighting the good fight against the Marlin and the sharks in the Gulf Stream with courage and love. He suffers a material defeat as he brings the skeleton of the Giant Marlin to the shore, but his material defect is transmuted into a spiritual and moral triumph and that provides a secure place against the all pervasive *Nada* of life.

## WORKS CITED

Hemingway Ernest, *In Our Time*. New York : Charles Scribner's Sons, 1930 (First pub. New York : Boni and Liveright, 1925).

——, *The Sun Also Rises*. New York : Charles Scribner's Sons, 1926.

——, *A Farewell to Arms*. New York : Charles Scribner's Sons, 1937 (First pub. 1929).

——, *Death in the Afternoon*. London : Jonathan Cape, 1956 (First pub. 1932).

——, *To Have and Have Not*. New York : Charles Scribner's Sons, 1937.

——, *The Fifth Column and the First Forty Nine Stories*. New York : Charles Scribner's Sons, 1938.

——, *For Whom the Bell Tolls*. New York : Charles Scribner's Sons, 1940.

——, *Across the River and into the Trees*. New York : Charles Scribner's Sons, 1950.

——, *The Old Man and the Sea*. New York : Charles Scribner's Sons, 1952.

——, *The Enduring Hemingway* : An Anthology of a *Lifetime in Literature*. New York : Scribner's Sons, 1971. Cited as *EH*.

## SELECT BIBLIOGRAPHY

Back, Melvin, "Hemingway : The Matador and the Crucified", *Modern American Fiction*, ed. A. Walton Lctz. New York : Oxford Univ. Press, 1963, pp. 201-14.

Barker, Carlos, *Ernest Hemingway : A Life Story*. New York : Charles Scribner's Sons, 1969.

——, *Ernest Hemingway : The Writer as Artist*. Princeton, New Jersey : Princeton University Press, 1971.

Benson, Jackson J., *Hemingway... The Writer's Art of Self-Defence*. Minneapolis : Univ. of Minnesota Press, 1969.

Donne, John, *The Poems of John Donne*, ed. Sir Herbert Grierson. London : Oxford Univ. Press, 1964 (First pub. 1933).

Eastman, Mak, "Bull in the Afternoon", *Ernest Hemingway : The Man and this Work*, ed. J.K.M. McCaffery. New York : The World Publishing Co., 1950, pp. 66-75.

Lewis, Robert W. Jr., *Hemingway on Love*. Austin and London : University of Texas Press, 1965.

Maurois, Andre, "Ernest Hemingway", *Hemingway and His Critics : An International Anthology*, ed. Carlos Baker. New York : Hill and Wang, 1965, pp. 38-54.

Paolini, Pier Francesco, "The Hemingway of the Major Works", *Hemingway and His Critics : An International Anthology,* ed. Carlos Baker. New York : Hill and Wang, 1966, pp. 131-44.

Rama Rao, P.G., *Ernest Hemingway : A Study in Narrative Technique*. New Delhi : S. Chand and Co. Ltd., 1980.

——, "With Grace Under Pressure", *Ernest Hemingway : Critiques of Four Major Novels*, ed. Carlos Baker.

Spilka, Mark, "The Death of Love in *The Sun Also Rises*", *Hemingway and His Critics : An International Anthology*, ed. Carlos Baker. New York : Hill and Wang, 1966, pp. 80-92.

Young, Philip, *Ernest Hemingway : A Reconsideration*. Univ. Park and London : The Pennysylvania State Univ. Press, 1966.

# 8

# *The Torrents of Spring* and Anxiety of Influence

*—Rama Kundu*

> "He most honours my style who learns under it to destroy the teacher" —*Whitman*

HAROLD BLOOM speaks of the "dialectic that governs the relations of poets as poets" (Bloom 25), by which he implies the fructifying rebellion or departure ("swerve" is his term) that the ephebe strikes in order to wrench himself free from the precursor's influence. Considered in this light, Hemingway's *The Torrents of Spring* (1926) may offer useful insight into a particular phase in the process of his artistic development. Thus *The Torrents of Spring*, Hemingway's second book and comparatively minor work, which was received with blame and praise in adequate measures, and has been almost forgotten by posterity, could still be an interesting study for the Hemingway critic; because it sheds light on the author in the making, the young writer's struggle to get over the influence of an elder precursor, and to find some breakthrough for himself, some literary form and style which should be essentially his own.

Hemingway's first commercially published book[1] *In Our Time* (1925) had been enthusiastically applauded and endorsed by Sherwood Anderson, an established American writer of the time, whose influence upon Hemingway was obvious in this book. But when Anderson said, "Mr. Hemingway is young, strong, full of laughter, and he can write" (Quoted by Meyers 13), little did he anticipate that the same laughter and writing skill should be turned on him, and so soon, in the very next book of Hemingway. Soon afterwards he wrote, in ten days according to his own claim, a hilarious parody, openly ridiculing Anderson's *Dark Laughter* (1925), the best-seller of the previous year, which shocked many of his contemporaries as also delighted some.

After so many years, and without reference to the immediate backdrop of or the impulse behind *The Torrents of Spring*, it is possible to mistake the book as an absurd rambling without a 'story' as such, and with too many funny touches the number and representatives of which could very well verge on boredom. But in 1926 Hemingway's readers could immediately recognize behind the parody the original target, and could read the story as an act of dethroning a popular fashion of the day.

Sherwood Anderson (1876-1941) not only represented this fashion; he had also become one of its trendsetters by the time Hemingway started writing. Anderson became famous with *Winesburg, Ohio* (1919) which had won exceeding popularity among young people throughout the country. *Dark Laughter*, which followed in 1925 had become a bestseller. Anderson's stories were supposed to be incomparable for mid Western life and character, infused with tenderness. Though Anderson was deprecated by later critics for sentimentality, he had, nevertheless, influenced such writers as Hemingway, Wolfe, Steinbeck, Faulkner, among others. In the early twenties his stories appealed to many young people, though when they reread him several years later, found him embarrassingly adolescent and quite outmoded. Still he helped a generation to grow up. Anderson's flaws — an unchanging style, lack of many-sidedness, slow prose, imperfect use of words in spite of his professed love for words — were balanced by his positive qualities. As Hansen puts it admiringly : "He...gives you the impression that he sees a bit beyond this external covering which buries men. He tries to dig down under the veneer of conventions" (76). Anderson's sensitive depictions of poverty and eccentricity, his simple style with its colloquial rhythms and matter-of-fact mid-Western sentences, opened new perspectives to twentieth century literature and influenced a wide range of American writers.

Anderson's *Dark Laughter* which is commonly acknowledged as the original text for Hemingway's Parody, is the story of one John Stockton who gets tired of his newspaper job, drifts in an open boat down the Illinois and Mississippi rivers, takes the fake name Bruce Dudley and joins as a factory worker in his native town. Here he gets involved with his employer's wife and runs away with her. This is the story in a nutshell. Narrated in the characteristic Andersonian style — a mixture of simplicity, soft rhetoric, and sentimentalism — the story also underscores a contrast between the white and the 'negro.' Anderson tries to hammer in the message, in the sentimental primitivistic 'Noble Savage' tradition (like Lawrence romanticizing the Hopi in his *Mornings in Mexico*) that the white man has been corrupted by civilization, and it is only the Negro with his 'Dark Laughter', who has escaped this corruption by means of his scorn for the white man's scruples.

Intertextual echoes are only too clearly audible in *The Torrents of Spring* which came out in the following spring, and in which Hemingway made a devastating mockery of *Dark Laughter*. This is evident from the very start. A comparison of even the openings of the two texts would bear evidence to Hemingway's intention of ridiculing and the consequent hilarious effect achieved through parody.

A (for Anderson) : Sponge...had a wife who got drunk with him sometimes on paydays.

H (for Hemingway) : Scripps O'Neil, a worker in the pump factory "with his wife in Mancelona often got drunk" (22).

A : Sponge had a daughter whom he playfully called Bugs Martin.

H : "Scripps had a daughter whom he playfully called Lousy O'Neil (Both Lousy and Bugs implying small but annoying insects).

A : "Time very soon to push the windows up. Spring would be soon coming now" (quoted by Garnett, 'Introduction' 12).

H : The opening sentences : "Yogi Johnson stood looking out of the window of a big pump factory in Michigan. Spring would soon be here." The comic twist comes in the following sentence : "Could it be that what this writing fellow Hutchinson had said, 'If winter comes can spring be far behind?' would be true again this year? Yogi Johnson wondered."

The mockery starts even earlier with the very title.[2] Hemingway's first section is titled 'Red and Black Laughter.' A Negro's laugh echoes an Indian war-hoop at chatper-endings.[3] The phrase "dark laughter of the negro" (115) occurs once, as Yogi is thrown out of the Indian club, to indicate mysterious hostility. This may be seen as contrast to the laughter of the group of Negro women who watch the development between Bruce and Aline, say nothing, and laugh; laughter is their speech. "The air on the hill top was filled with laughter, dark laughter" (Garnett 'Introduction' 14). Again, Hemingway's title is taken from a novel by Turgenev whose *Sportsman's Sketches* Anderson admired as "the sweetest thing in all literature" (Baker 40). Turgenev's *Torrents of Spring* tells of love forsaken in springtime lust. The motif of 'spring was coming on' runs through *Dark Laughter*. A similar motif recurs mockingly in *The Torrents of Spring*.[4] The coming of the spring wind in Dark Laughter synchronizes with the growing love between Bruce and Aline. Here the spring wind first warms up Scripps O'Neil who goes from waitress to waitress in quick succession[5] while he is also watched by some black face. Yogi Johnson wonders at his lack of desire before the "chinook" wind, but is finally stirred to desire by the naked squaw. In *Dark Laughter* the reporter leaves his highbrow wife to come away to a remote town and join a wheel factory in the job of painting wheels. Here Scripps, who sells his 'stories' to Loriner, is deserted by his lowbrow wife and comes to a pump factory where they work to cover the pump with snow. The stereotype of the Noble Savage is shattered as Yogi is thrown out from the Indian club for being an outsider, to the accompaniment of derisive "dark laughter" (115). There are many such details and moments when imitation is twisted and lifted into hilarity.

The stylistic parodies are indeed brilliant. Hemingway mocks the superficial interior monologues of Anderson with superb effect. Rourke thus comments on Anderson's monologue : "the unwarranted personal intrusion — the vestiges of the monologue where the monologue has no place" (230). Hemingway exploits this habit to lead to much mirth and amusement. Hemingway caricatures Anderson's verbal nuances and his naivete by means of characters who are inarticulate, confused, and amusing with their "wonderments." A fine example is Scripps' thoughts about telegraphers : "Scripps was at a loss. What sort of chap was this telegrapher? What sort of men went in for telegraphy? Were they like composers? Were they like artists? Were they like writers? Were they like the advertising men who write the ads in our national weeklies? Or were they like Europeans, drawn and wasted by the war, their best years behind them?..." (38). Yogi, after being thrown out by the Indians, ponders : "Where had he been? Had he been in an Indian club? What was it all about? Was this the end?" (120) It has been noted how this sounds very much like "Anderson's interior tremolo" (Baker 41). As Quennell rightly says, Hemingway's characters "express their deepest feelings in the charactertistic Andersonian telegraphese" (87). Hemingway recaptures Anderson's mannerisms to perfection : the short sentences, repetitious thoughts and expressions, the Andersonian mood of watching the commonplace facts of life with a boyish sort of amazement in slow and simple prose. In Meyers's words, it is "a devastating mockery of the naive repetition and superficial psychology in Anderson's novel" (14). Also there are moments of hilarity concocted from the literarily worn and false; for example, Yogi on the poet "Hutchinson (21), or Scripps on Windermere and Scotland, or discussing literature with Mandy, the waitress.

Hemingway's use of intertext as a device for deriding provoked mixed response among critics. Many of his contemporaries and later critics found it in bad taste. For example, Horace Liveright (the original for Lorimer), who had published his first book, had been shocked at reading the TS and rejected it on the ground that to publish it would be "horribly cruel to Anderson" (Meyers 14). In spite of excellent touches the book was held to be "an embarrassment", "an attack on former friends" (Baker 42; 40), "the first of many instances when Hemingway repaid kindness with malice" (Meyers 14), an instance of ingratitude (Hansen, quoted by Meyers 15). On the other hand some critics seemed to feel that Anderson's feeble fiction deserved this witty and well-executed condemnation. Carlos Baker defends it as a joke not meant to be mean; he justifies it on the ground that "when a man like Sherwood who was capable of great things wrote something rotten it was Ernest's obligation to call him on it.... Since the book was not intended as a personal attack, the tougher it was, the better" (204, 212). Garnett in his 'Introduction' held that Hemingway was not parodying the story but the ideas behind it, and the falsity of the author's approach that the Negroes were nearer Nature than white men. Allen Tate found the parody a better book than *Dark Laughter* and called the work "a small masterpiece of American fiction" (78). Of course Tate noted the element of personal aggression; but he found it amusing here.[6] Garnett even considered it as enjoyable as Lear's Nonsense Verses which made "the reader exhausted by too much laughter" (80).

Neither the defence nor the attack, however, seems to adequately explain Hemingway's attack on Anderson. It is Peter Quennell who seems to provide an important hint when he points out the element of self-parody in the novel, that "it is also a satire on Anderson's method as Hemingway himself has seen fit to adapt it" (87). Garnett has also noted that "one finds him continually laughing at himself" (83) in this novel. A possible explanation of Hemingway's parody of Anderson may lie in this elaborate self-parody,[7] which, read closely, appears to disclose the young writer's (the ephebe of Bloom) anxiety to wrench himself free from a precursor's influence.

That Hemingway was considerably influenced by Anderson is beyond question. As Brian Way claims, "His debt to Anderson was enormous, though his acknowledgement of it was almost always disingenuous and grudging" (159). It was an early influence which was likely to have left a strong and lasting impression. David Seed (19) confirms this : "...Anderson who Hemingway read extensively before he left for Europe. Indeed, Hemingway told Scott Fitzerald in 1925 that Winesburg, Ohio had been his first model." His early story, "My Old Man", his first story to win a literary honour, "was influenced by Anderson" (Baker 17). Baker points out Hemingway's mixed reaction to this spell as he emphasizes Hemingway's "avid admiration" for the works of Anderson "whom he claimed as model and was to deny as master" (14). Quennell also stresses this dual response : "Mr. Hemingway, who...had been under the spell of Anderson's method...was apparently was both enchanted and disabused...." (80). Meyers's perceptive comment throws light on the process from enchantment to rebellion; "Hemingway's ability to parody Anderson", Meyers says, "reveals how well he had learned and then rejected the lesson of the master" (14). Indeed, he parodies a style too near his own.

*The Torrents of Spring* thus emerges as the mixed product of the author's learning from a precursor and unlearning him. The unlearning, as it required as effort on the author's part, may explain his aggressive stance. One feels Hemingway is being aggressive here with a decision. Even as he admits that Anderson might find it "a lousy, snotty book", he insists on sincerity and the hope that Anderson's thoughts and style would be significantly improved by reading the strictures of a younger colleague. Considering the author's personal debt to Anderson this seems like rude ingratitude.[8] At the same time, it is interesting to note how Hemingway tries to enlist the prestige of quotes from Fielding which, however, do not always appear appropriate.[9]

Again, it may be noted that Hemingway was supported in this case mainly by some younger writers of the time who may also have shared a more or less similar anxiety.[10] To quote the introductory note to *100 Great American Novels* : "...few American writers have had greater influence on other writers both in their own times and in later generations than Sherwood Anderson" (19). How remarkable and sometimes dangerous the influence was may be guessed from Scott-Fitzerald's observation : "The American admirers of Anderson proceeded to imitate Anderson's lapses from that difficult simplicity they are unable to understand", and, as a result, the "disorganization" brings their books to a "timely and unregrettable doom" (313-14). The blame Scott-Fitzerald attributes to Anderson for adversely affecting his admirers may perhaps offer an explanation why Hemingway, in his very second book, — and in spite of his debts to Anderson — exhibited such an anxiety to disengage himself from Anderson's influence. Seen in this perspective it also becomes easier to understand Hemingway's imitations and distortions of Anderson's text.

Faulkner, however, distanced himself from the above trend and paid his unqualified tribute to Anderson :

"He was the father of my generation of American writers and the tradition of American writing which our successors will carry on" (368). Nevertheless, the tribute itself gives us a clue to Hemingway's 'ingratitude.' One may recall here Harold Bloom's analogy of the battle between strong equals, father and son, Laius and Oedipus, in order to describe the "exhaustions" of the latecomer *vis-a-vis* the precursor, the two "mighty opposites" (12). Here we have a case exemplifying this battle where the sons get arrayed against the father, which is, according to Bloom, a repeated historical and literary phenomenon (12). Bloom relates the latecomer's "exhaustions" to his anxious realisation that "to be enslaved by any precursor's system is to be inhibited from creativity by an obsessive reasoning and comparing of one's own work to the precursor's" (Bloom 29). Did Hemingway want to shake off this spell of a precursor, which could be "a disease of self-consciousness" (Bloom 29)? And since on such an occasion to be judicious is to be weak, and to compare exactly and fairly, is to be not elect (Bloom 19), Hemingway chose the other alternative, — to be strong and unfair. Bloom claims that "the history of fruitful poetic influence...is a history of anxiety and self-saving caricature, of distortion, of perverse wilful revisionism" (30). Hemingway illustrates this process by wilfully, mockingly, perversely rewriting his precursor in *The Torrents of Spring*.

However, it may seem intersting to note, and ironical too, that even after this, the influence of Anderson continued to affect Hemingway's theme and style. Sheridan Baker acknowledged this by pointing out, "From Anderson, Hemingway learned to see his own central subject : loneliness against the world" (14). The Andersonian element also continued to mould his style as Cyril Connolly stressed in his review of *To Have and Have Not*, written eleven years later : "Hemingway is the victim of his style" in this book; and this "style was originally formed by two influences...'Huckleberry Finn' and Gertrude Stein-Sherwood Anderson. It was a reaction against the verbose highbrow style of the literary mandarins...and aimed at complete simplicity and co-ordination between the written word and the violent emotions behind it" (226).[11] This is the style that reached such perfection in *The Old Man and the Sea* (after another twenty-six years), such poignancy in his major mature works. Hemingway, it appears, could never completely shake off his first model. He continued to carry the Andersonian heritage in his short, abrupt sentences, weighted with inarticulate masculinity, vibrant with the tenor of spoken speech.[12]

Finally, it may be amusing to recall that nobody may be immune to similar attacks from posterity. Thus Philip Roth stuffed his *The Great American Novel* (1972) with burlesques and parodies which had wide range of victims, and a high point was a parody of Ernest Hemingway doing a parody of *Moby Dick*.

## NOTES

1. Hemingway's first book *Three Stories and Ten Poems* was privately published in 1923 with 300 copies; *In Our Time* was also privately published in 1924 with lower-case title and 170 copies.

2. In fact, from the very dedication Hemingway assumes an aggressive posture of self-assertion. Sardonically he dedicated to H.L. Mencken who had committed the unforgivable fault of adversely reviewing *In Our Time*, and to S. Stanwood Menken "who stood for everything Mencken hated."
3. *TTOS*, 14; 25; 29; 66; 81; 113; 115; 116; 119; 120; 121.
4. *TTOS*, 21; 95; 96; 97; 137; 153; 154.
5. "Hemingway remakes Anderson's internal stirrings into a spring time thaw at a Petosky pump factory and leading Scripps O'Neil from one waitress to another" and then "out into the night after a naked squaw" (Baker, S. 40).
6. "Mr. Hemingway has for some time been in the habit of throwing pebbles at the great — which recalls Mr. Pope's couplet about Dennis. The habit was formed in *The Torrents of Spring*, where it amusing" (Allen Tate 95).
7. Scripps is a reporter-cum-hackwriter; Windermer was also the name of Hemingway's Simmer home at Walloon Lake.
8. Harry Hansen : "Anderson trumpeted loudly (for Hemingway), and now Hemingway pays him back by making him the principal butt of his parody" (76).
9. Sheridan Baker : "He quotes Fielding on the Ridiculous, and either misses Fielding's point or cannot illustrate it — or thinks the statement itself is fusty and antique...and his Ridiculous becomes ridiculous" (41).
10. Anderson had also been the object of ridicule in Wyndham Lewis's *Paleface.*

    Quennell welcomed the book for "an astringency much needed at the present time" (88).
11. Delmore Schwartz, the American short story writer, noted : "he has of course learned a method of style from them (Stein-Anderson)" (245).
12. Constance Rourke : "These tales of Anderson...restore an element that had been dominant in the long American tradition, that of speech : their air of improvisation is not accidental; many of them are told as if spoken" (230).

    Ironically, Anderson and Hemingway have come to be bracketed together in later times as "deliberate practitioners of black humour" in American literature (Brom Weber 370).

    Anderson had continued to operate as a major influence even in the forties. As Blair and Hill put it : "Beginning in 1919, when Sherwood Anderson stocked Winesburg, Ohio with the abnormal, put-upon folk who were bedeviled by complexes and phobias, psychology — almost all of it Freudian — had become the "in" thing among the literati..." (450).

## WORKS CTIED

Anderson, S., *Dark Laughter*, Chicago : Boni & Liveright, 1925.

Baker, Carlos, *Ernest Hemingway*, Qyoted by Meyers, "Introduction",

*Hemingway : The Critical Heritage*. Boston : Routledge & Kegan Paul, 1982.

Baker, Sheridan, *Ernest Hemingway*. N.Y. : Holt, Rinehart & Winston, 1967.

Blair, W., Hill, H., *American Humor*. N.Y. : O.U.P., 1978.

Bloom, H., *The Anxiety of Influence* (1973). N.Y. : O.U.P., Paperback, 1975.

Connolly, C., New Statesman and the Nation, 16 Oct., 1937, *Critical Heritage*, 226-29.

Faulkner, W., "The Paris Review Interview", *The Theory of the American Novel.*

Fitzerald, F. Scott, "How to Waste Material : a Note on My Generation", *The Theory of the American Novel*, (ed.) G. Perkins. N.Y. : Holt, Rinehart & Winston, 1970.

Garnett, D., "Introduction", *The Torrents of Spring* (1926). London, Jonathan Cape, 1964.

——, *The Critical Heritage.*

Hansen, H., "New York World", 30 May, 1926, *The Critical Heritage*, pp. 74-78.

Hemingway, E., *The Torrents of Spring*, 1964 edition.

Meyers, G., "Introduction", *The Critical Heritage*, pp. 1-62.

Quennell, P., *The Critical Heritage*, pp. 85-88.

Rourke, C., *American Humor*, N.Y., A Doubleday Anchor Book, 1931.

Schwartz, D., *The Critical Heritage*, pp. 243-56.

Seed, D., "The Picture of the Whole", *Ernest Hemingway : New Critical Essays*, (ed.) A.R. Lee. London : Vision and Barnes & Noble, 1983, pp. 13-35.

Tate, A., *The Critical Heritage*, pp. 78-79.

Weber, B., "The Misspellers", *The Comic Imagination in American Literature*, (Ed.) L.J. Rubin, New Jersey : Rutgers Univ. Press, 1973.

Way, B., "Hemingway the Intellectual : A Version of Modernism", Ernest Hemingway (Ed.) Lees, A.R.

*100 Great American Novels*, N.Y. : Signet Book, 1966.

# 9

# Symbolism in *The Sun Also Rises*

*—Ishteyaque Shams*

IT GOES without saying that Hemingway has been a very popular writer and his novels have attracted readers in a large and still larger number. His popularity is not conditioned so much by his descriptions of sex and violence, travels and adventures in his novels and stories as by something that lies hidden behind these descriptions. Truly enough, Hemingway is a writer of a lost generation, of an era of chaos and disillusionment, but his approach is neither defeatist nor negative in nature; instead, it is something vigorously optimistic and positive in spirit. As we go through his writings, his novels and short stories in particular, we do find that here is a writer who looks upon life as a kind of struggle and challenge, and who believes that in spite of all adverse situations it is always better to get destroyed than to accept defeat. Moreover, this import of Hemingway's works is heightened and made richer and more meaningful and significant by the manner in which he brings it out. What Hemingway seeks to tell us through his novels and short stories is indeed important, but far important is the way, the mode in which he tells it. It is generally said that Hemingway writes in a very plain, simple and austere kind of style and that there is nothing involved or complex or ambiguous as such about his writing. However, as I went through his novels, *The Sun Also Rises* in particular, I did realize that there was much to be explored and considered in order to be able to make a proper and adequate assessment of his linguistic capability. It was at this point that I thought of tracing out symbols in *The Sun Also Rises*.

It is not very easy to define a symbol, but it is also not very difficult to distinguish a symbol from an image. A symbol is also an image, but it is a kind of an image that has gained greater currency and a wider spectrum of interest. There are certain symbols that are conventional, archetypal or universal, but there are also certain other symbols that come to us as innovations. It is interesting to see that in Hemingway's novels we come across both the kinds of symbols. At the same time it would also be profitable to mention here that a consideration of symbols does necessarily involve a consideration of images too, because most of these images contribute to the totality of implication or suggestion that symbols stand for. It is precisely for this reason that besides symbols, I have also considered most of the important images too that figure in *The Sun Also Rises*.

Speaking of symbolism and irony together in his very illuminating essay entitled "Hemingway's Ambiguity : Symbolism and Irony", E.M. Halliday says :

> ...all perceptions are reducible finally to perceptions of likeness or perceptions of difference. Perhaps this offers a clue to the effectiveness of both symbolism and irony.... Symbolism does depend essentially on likeness, and irony on difference; and as artistic tools both are means of interpreting imaginatively, and with the flexibility of implication, a complex reality. Symbolism signifies through a harmony, irony through a discord : symbolism consolidates, irony complicates; symbolism synthesizes, irony analyzes.

Halliday does rightly point out that symbolism depends on the likeness of two or more than two objects, that it is a mode of perception, that as an artistic tool it seeks to interpret complex realities imaginatively, and that it works through harmony and synthesis.

It is in the context of Hemingway's use of images and symbols in his fictional works that we have to refer to what is known as his iceberg theory of language and presentation. In *Death in the Afternoon*, Hemingway writes :

> If a writer of prose knows enough about what he is writing about he may omit things that he knows and the reader, if the writer is writing truly enough, will have a feeling of those things as strongly as though the writer had stated them. The dignity of movement of an iceberg is due to only one-eighth of it being above water.

No doubt, Hemingway is a realist; no doubt, he maintains strict fidelity to realism, to the truthfulness of details and descriptions, and yet we find that his imagination, his artistic invention yields a kind of truth that is much higher than or superior to the realism or truthfulness of factual account. Carlos Baker speaks of the artist's grasp of the relationship between the temporal and the eternal, and says that this 'grasp is expressed, in his fiction, through the considered use of imaginative symbols.' With particular reference to Hemingway, Baker goes on to say :

> Most of these come, by way of the artist's imagination, from the visible material universe — the mountains and the plains, the rivers and the trees, the weather and the seasons, the land and the sea. To such natural images Hemingway has attached the strong emotional power of his artistic apprehension of them.... At the same time, Hemingway has generally managed to render with fidelity each of the natural objects or scenes precisely for what, in itself, it really is. As a result of their union with imagination and emotion, the various phenomena rise up as operative symbols in all his art. They become thereby not less real but more real than they are in themselves because of the double or triple significations with which they have been imbued.

There is indeed a peculiarly productive combination of the real and the imaginative, of realism and symbolism, of fact and suggestion, of statement and implication in Hemingway's novels.

Ernest Hemingway's first novel, *The Sun Also Rises*, was published in 1926, and, as we go through the book, it becomes unmistakably clear to us that the period of time that this book covers in respect of action is just one year, that is, 1925. In the post-First World War era, the world was rather returning to normalcy and the European economy was gradually picking up its desired tempo. It is a period of disarmament and peace treatises, of conferences on progress and co-operation, and indeed of growing stability. It was an era of guarded hope and happiness, for the threat of war, insurgency, revolution, or counter-revolution had nearly receded. Moreover, it was an era in which America had emerged as a powerful country, a country enjoying not merely political authority but also great industrial progress and economic boom. Nevertheless, what we find in *The Sun Also Rises*, or for that matter in Hemingway's other novels too, is an air of disenchantment, a climate of ennui or boredom, an atmosphere of morbidity, depression or futility that goes counter to the general physical condition of Europe. Naturally enough, in his essay on *The Sun Also Rises*, James T. Farrell comments : 'it may seem paradoxical that in such a period a novel of war disillusionment, nihilistic in outlook, should have become an international success' (Farrell 20). However, it is not at all difficult to explain this seeming paradox or contradiction if we examine the whole thing in the right perspective.

Perhaps all the people who had actually participated in war, or had been its victims in one way or another, were, quite understandably, disenchanted with life because of its horrors and brutalities. However, far more than physical injury, war had caused a kind of psychological crisis and moral degradation on account of which the post-war period was one of delicate and difficult adjustment with the realities of life. 'Hemingway', as Philip Young puts it, 'had deeply felt and understood what was in the wind' (Young 59). Jacob or Jake Barnes, the hero of *The Sun Also Rises*, has been rendered impotent on account of the injuries inflicted on him during the war, but, more or less, he has reconciled himself to the conditions of his life. As Barnes is moving about with Georgette, a prostitute, he has picked up accidentally, he asks her :

> 'What's the matter? You sick?'
> 'Yes.'
> 'Everybody's sick. I'm sick, too' (*SAR* 17).

According to Farrell, 'a re-examination of the character of disillusionment portrayed in *The Sun Also Rises* suggests that this mood had become a way of feeling and acting; in fact, a social habit' (Farrell 21). This mood of sickness or disenchantment with life, not unnaturally, prompted people to be rather nihilistic in their attitude and discard every form of middle-class respectability. And, not unexpectedly, Hemingway tries to express this mood through escapades, through a search for new sensations, through acts of calculated bravado, through drinking, fishing, bull-fighting and sexual exploits, through regular visits to clubs, cafés, hotels and restaurants. One of the titles of the present novel, Fiesta, is, as such, utterly significant.

In *The Sun Also Rises*, written in the first person, almost all the characters, except for Robert Cohn, look alike, are alike, and form a special group of their own. In several of its early editions, *The Sun Also Rises* had on its title page Gertrude Stein's famous statement : "You are all a lost generation." And, as Mark Spilka observes, in a broader sense, these characters are 'all disaffiliates, all men and women who have cut themselves off from conventional society and who have made Paris their permanent playground (Shapiro 245).

## II

The first striking image that we come across in *The Sun Also Rises* is that of emptiness, an image that is rendered in various ways and forms and which is very much in consonance with the general mood or temper of the novel. In Chapter 6 of the present novel Hemingway gives us a picture of empty barges being towed down the current, and it is significant that Jake Barnes watches their movement on the Seine :

> Brett had not been in the bar either, and so I looked for her upstairs on my way out, and took a taxi for the Café Select. Crossing the Seine I saw a string of barges being towed empty down the current, riding high, the bargemen at the sweeps as they came towards the bridge (36).

And later in the same Chapter Jake Barnes goes to a café which has very few people inside it and where Jake notices a pile of empty saucers lying on a table before Harvey Stone :

> No matter what café in Montparnasse you ask a taxi-driver to bring you to from the right bank of the river, they always take you to the Rotonde. Ten years from now it will probably be the Dôme. It was near enough, anyway. I walked past the sad tables of the Rotonde to the Select. There were a few people inside at the bar, and outside, alone, sat Harvey Stone. He had a pile of saucers in front of him...(36).

This feeling of emptiness is indeed a pervading presence in *The Sun Also Rises.*

It is indeed remarkable to see that even while the Spanish town of Pamplona is getting ready for the fiesta and the place is bracing itself up for the occasion, Hemingway speaks of the empty stands of the amphitheatre surrounding the bull-ring. He says : 'standing at the edge of the smooth rolled sand you could look up in the empty stands and see old women sweeping out the boxes' (115). Similarly after the fiesta is over, as Jake Barnes, Bill Gorton and Mike Campbell are about to leave for Pamplona, Jake looks at the empty town square which, only a day earlier, was bristling with activity and looking colourful and resplendent in the glow of festive celebrations :

> The fiesta was finished. I woke about nine o'clock, had a bath, dressed, and went downstairs. The square was empty and there were no people on the streets. A few children were picking up rocket-sticks in the square. The cafés were just opening and the waiters were carrying out the comfortable wicker chairs and arranging them around the marble-topped tables in the shade of the arcade. They were sweeping the streets and sprinkling them with a hose (174).

And, likewise, as Bill Gorton is leaving Bayonne for Paris by train, Jake watches the empty rail-tracks that do seem to hold out to him a peculiar kind of significance :

> He went in through the gate to the train. The porter went ahead with the bags. I watched the train pull out. Bill was at one of the windows. The window passed, the rest of the train passed, and the tracks were empty (177).

The empty stands, the empty square and the empty rail-tracks — they are all of a piece, suggesting the futility and meaninglessness of human life.

It is in a similar vein that, once again, we get an image of empty coffee-glasses and cognac-glasses in Chapter 16 of the present novel :

> He sat down and looked at her across the table. I went out. The hard-eyed people at the bull-fighter table watched me go. It was not pleasant. When I came back and looked in the café, twenty minutes later, Brett and Pedro Romero were gone. The coffee-glasses and the three empty cognac-glasses were on the table. A waiter came with a cloth and picked up the glasses and mopped off the table (144).

Brett Ashley and the bull-fighter, Pedro Romero, are steadily moving closer and closer to each other. For Jake Barnes this is surely an interesting development, since he knows that this growing closeness is as much incompatible as any such proximity between listlessness and life, between experience and sheer youthfulness.

However these images of emptiness, signifying loss, decay or separation, are generally followed by the images of cleansing, mopping up or sweeping, and they have their own bearing as much on the theme of the novel as on the given situations and the nature or attitude of individual characters.

Quite a few of the other images that we get in *The Sun Also Rises* relate chiefly to Robert Cohn and bring out the essential nature of his character. Cohn is a Jew 'a member, through his father, of one of the richest Jewish family in New York, and through his mother of one of the oldest' (9), and was 'once middleweight boxing champion of Princeton' (9). He has been a football player, a tennis player, a bridge palyer, and, besides, a bit of a novelist too, for, as the author says, he 'wrote a novel,... although it was a very poor novel' (11). However, what is really most relevant about him is that though he moves in the company of Jake Barnes, Brett Ashley and others in Paris as well as in Spain, really speaking, he is not one of them. His immaturity, his lack of perceptiveness, his wayward youthfulness and his sickening ways of behaviour are brought into sharp focus only to be contradistinguished from the manners and mannerisms of the other major characters of this novel. The very fact that Hemingway speaks of him in terms of his 'suitcase with (the) football things in it' (48), his 'polo shirt' (149) and his 'boxing fits and crying' (148) suggests that here is a character who is not at all sure of himself and who, as such, cannot make a proper assessment of the prevailing situation. He claims to be ardently in love with Brett Ashley; he looks at her as 'his compatriot must have looked when he saw the promised land' (22), and yet the fact of the matter is that he has 'never been in love in his life' (12). He is a bit of an imposter; even so, when he learns from Jake Barnes that Brett Ashley has gone off with the bull-fighter, Pedro Romero, he flies into a rage and hits him hard :

> I swung at him and he ducked. I saw his face duck sideways in the light. He hit me and I sat down on the pavement. As I started to get on my feet he hit me twice. I went down backwards under a table. I tried to get up and felt I did not have any legs. I felt I must get on my feet and try and hit him. Mike helped me up. Someone poured a carafe of water on my head. Mike had an arm around me and I found I was sitting on a chair. Mike was pulling at my ears.
>
> 'I say, you were cold', Mike said.
>
> 'Where the hell were you?'
>
> 'Oh, I was round.'
>
> 'You didn't want to mix in it?'
>
> 'He knocked Mike down, too,' Edna said.
>
> 'He didn't knock me out.'
>
> Mike said, 'I just lay there.'
>
> 'Does this happen every night at your fiestas?' Edna asked.
>
> 'Wasn't that Mr. Cohn?' (146).

Robert Cohn's polo shirt and his phantom suitcase, observes Mark Spilka in his essay entitled 'The Death of Love in *The Sun Also Rises*', remind us (immediately) of one of those dreamlike fantasies by the Czech genius Franz Kafka, in which trunks and youthful clothes are symbols of arrested development (Shapiro 251). In the course of one of his authorial comments Hemingway himself says that there is 'a funny short of undergraduate quality' (39) about Cohn, and Harvey Stone describes Cohn's case as one of "arrested development" (38).

Robert Cohn is an odd character, almost an absurd character, and yet he occupies a key position in the novel. He is, as Mark Spilka puts it, 'the last chivalric hero, the last defender of an outworn faith, and his function is to illustrate its present folly — to show us, through the absurdity of his behaviour, that romantic love is dead, that one of the great guiding codes of the past no longer operates (Shapiro 241).

If Jake Barnes and his friends are by and large disillusioned people, rootless and shaky and rather lost; and if Robert Cohn is a false romantic hero, then Pedro Romero is a character who is rooted in the Spanish tradition and soil. He is a simple and unassuming person : there is, as the novelist himself says, 'nothing conceited or braggartly about him' (133), and though only nineteen years old, he does have his own sense of self-confidence and dignity to keep him utterly unruffled. He is a trained and accomplished bull-fighter with a handsome face and smokes only cigars because they form 'part of his system of authority' (142) and make him 'seem older' (142). He takes on Brett Ashley as slowly and as surely as he takes on bulls inside the ring, and even though he is thrashed repeatedly by Robert Cohn, he remains undefeated both physically and spiritually. Pedro Romero stands for virility, and personifies everything good that would survive the failure of Jake Barnes and his associates.

As we go through *The Sun Also Rises*, we find that there are certain images in the novel, the figurative as well as the descriptive image, that present to us an integrated picture of happiness, growth and fruitfulness. The spirit of freedom and gaiety that is associated with 'fishing' in the Irati river of Burguete in Spain is the first case in point :

> We stayed five days at Burguete and had good fishing. The nights were cold and the days were hot, and there was always a breeze even in the heat of the day. It was hot enough so that it felt good to wade in a cold stream, and the sun dried you when you came out and sat on the bank. We found a stream with a pool deep enough to swim in. In the evenings we played three-handed bridge with an Englishman named Harris, who had walked over from Saint Jean Pied de Port and was stopping at the inn for the fishing. He was very pleasant and went with us twice to the Irati river (97).

Similarly, the way Hemingway describes the ritualistic bull-fight and the fiesta makes us aware of the fact that in spite of all depression and despair and morbidity, life does have a built-in mechanism of its own to assert and reassert itself over adverse situations :

> The fiesta was really started. It kept up day and night for seven days. The dancing kept up, the drinking kept up, the noise went on. The things that happened could only have happened during a fiesta. Everything became quite unreal finally and it seemed as though nothing could have any consequences. It seemed out of place to think of consequences during the fiesta. All during the fiesta you had the feeling, even when it was quiet, that you had to shout any remark to make it heard. It was the same feeling about any action. It was a fiesta and it went on for seven days (118-19).

It is important to note that it is only during the fiesta that we come across happy interludes in the novel : before and after the fiesta it is all emptiness.

It is, more or less, in a similar vein that we encounter the goat image in Chapter 12 of the present novel. Significantly enough, this image is introduced immediately after the description of hard wind blowing and roofs cracking in a foul and troublesome weather. Jake is delighted to see a goat hopping up and down on a cart in the morning following the stormy night :

> When I woke in the morning I went to the window and looked out. It had cleared and there were no clouds on the mountains. Outside under the window were some carts and an old diligence, the wood of the roof cracked and split by the weather. It must have been left from the days before the motor-buses. A goat hopped up on one of the carts and then to the roof of the diligence. He jerked his head at the other goats below and when I waved at him he bounded down (87).

The goat, it is so very clear to us, stands for energy and agility, for hope and joy. And, quite understandably, it is in order to give us a picture of growth and fulfilment that, in he following passage, Hemingway describes the Burguete landscape, as the tourists view it :

> We walked on the road between the thick trunks of the old beeches and the sunlight came through the leaves in light patches on the grass. The trees were big, and the foliage was thick but it was not gloomy. There was no undergrowth, only the smooth grass, very green and fresh, and the big grey trees well spaced as though it were a park.... There were wild strawberries growing on the sunny side of the ridge in a little clearing in the trees (90-91).

All these images, either relating to sport, holidaying or Nature, signify such forces as have their own revitalizing effect.

## III

It is significant to remember that some of these images function as symbols, or at least have symbolic dimensions. 'Rain' is one of the symbols in *The Sun Also Rises*, and while usually rain stands for life, for fertility, for vegetation and growth, in the present novel it stands for minor destruction or dislocation, for gloom and bad weather :

> In the morning it was raining. A fog had come over the mountains from the sea. You could not see the tops of the mountains. The plateau was dull and gloomy, and the

> shapes of the trees and houses were changed. I walked out beyond the town to look at the weather. The bad weather was coming over the mountains from the sea. The flags in the square hung wet from the white poles and the banners were wet and hung dump against the front of the houses, and in beween the steady drizzle the rain came down and drove everyone under the arcades and made pools of water in the square, and the streets wet and dark and deserted... (130).

It is true, as we find, that the rain causes some disturbance to the fiesta : nevertheless, the show goes on and on 'without any pause' (130).

As we go through the present novel, we see that the game of poker dice has its own symbolical value and that the context in which it is described does impart to it a specific kind of meaningfulness :

> So we rolled poker dice out of a deep leather dice-cup. Bill was out first roll. Mike lost to me and handed the bartender a hundred-franc note. The whiskies were twelve francs apiece. We had another round and Mike lost again. Each time he gave the bartender a good tip. In a room off the bar there was a good jazz band playing. It was a pleasant bar. We had another round. I went out on the first roll with four kings. Bill and Mike rolled. Mike won the first roll with four jacks. Bill won the second. On the final roll Mike had three kings and let them stay. He handed the dice-cup to Bill. Bill rattled them and rolled, and there were three kings, an ace, and a queen (175).

The fiesta at Pamplona is over; the tourists are in a mood to leave the place, and before leaving for their destinations, Jake Barnes, Mike Campbell and Bill Gorton play the game of poker dice. It is not at all difficult to see that while the three kings stand for Jake Barnes, Mike Campbell and Bill Gorton, the ace stands for Robert Cohn and the queen for Brett Ashley. Moreover, Campbell's final victory in the game of poker dice anticipates his ultimate victory in life too, for even though Robert Cohn keeps on shadowing Brett and the bull-fighter, Pedro

Romero, takes her away from Mike, finally she would return to him alone.

Similarly, the picture of a Khaki-clad mounted policeman directing traffic does also work as a symbol :

> Downstairs we came out through the first-floor dining-room to the street. A waiter went for a taxi. It was hot and bright. Up the street was a little square with trees and grass where there were taxis parked. A taxi came up the street, the waiter hanging out at the side. I tipped him and told the driver where to drive, and got in beside Brett. The driver started up the street. I settled back. Brett moved close to me. We sat close against each other. I put my arm around her and she rested against me comfortably. It was very hot and bright, and the houses looked sharply white. We turned out on to the Gran Via.
>
> 'Oh, Jake,' Brett said, 'we could have had such a damned good time together.'
>
> Ahead was a mounted policeman in khaki directing traffic. He raised his baton. The car slowed suddenly pressing Brett against me (189).

The policeman directs the traffic by raising his baton, but it appears to Jake Barnes and Brett Ashley who are inside a taxi that the policeman does so in a rather unconcerned manner. This unconcern on the policemna's part, in a way, symbolizes the indifferent elemental forces that, according to them, govern human activities.

It is indeed amazing that in an unobtrusive manner Hemingway introduces two minor symbols in *The Sun Also Rises* in the form of Brett Ashley's trembling hands (141) and the scars of arrow wounds (50) on the back of Count Mippipopolous. We see, without any ambiguity whatsoever, that while Brett Ashley's trembling hands symbolize her inner weakness or brokenness, the scars of arrow wounds on the Count's back represent the widespread adverse impact that war has made on the human psyche.

'Hemingway', says James T. Farrell, 'is a writer of limited vision, one who has no broad and fertile perspectives on life' (Farrell 22). And still *The Sun Also Rises*, is Hemingway's *Waste Land*, and Jake Barnes is his Fisher King. This may be a wild surmise or a sweeping generalization, but Philip Young says something in this connection that is indeed very useful. He says : '...once again here is the protagonist gone impotent, and his land gone sterile. Eliot's London is Hemingway's Paris, where spiritual life in general, and Jake's sexual life in particular, are alike impoverished. Prayer breaks down and falls, a knowledge of traditional distinctions between good and evil is largely lost, copulation is morally neutral and, cut off from the past chiefly by the spiritual disaster of the war, life has become mostly meaningless. "What shall we do?" is the same constant question, to which the answer must be, again, "Nothing." To hide it, instead of playing chess one drinks, mechanically and always. Love is a possibility only for the two who cannot love; once again homosexuality intensifies this atmosphere of sterility; once more the Fisher King is also a man who fishes' (Young 59-60). However, in Eliot's *Waste Land*, Philip Young goes on to say, 'a message of salvation comes out of the life-giving rain which falls on western civilization. In Hemingway's waste land there is fun, but there is no hope. No rain falls on Europe this time...' (Young 60).

In his turn Mark Spilka observes that Hemingway designs 'an extensive parable' (Shapiro 239) in *The Sun Also Rises*. In this novel, Spilka further says, 'his protagonists are deliberately shaped as allegorical figures : Jake Barnes and Brett Ashley are two lovers desexed by the war; Robert Cohn is the false knight who challenges their despair; while Romero, the stalwart bull-fighter, personifies the good life which will survive their failure. Of course, these characters are not abstractions in the text; they are realized through the most concrete style in American fiction, and their larger meaning is implied by their response to immediate situations. But the implications are there, the parable is at work in every scene, and its presence lends unity and depth to the whole novel (Shapiro 239).

It is important to realize that the true allegorical or symbolical significance of *The Sun Also Rises* lies contained in its title. This title has been taken from *Ecclesiastes* of the *Old Testament*, and the relevant lines are as follows :

> The words of the Preacher, the son of David, king in Jerusalem.
>
> Vanity of vanities, saith the Preacher, vanity of vanities; all is vanity. What profit hath a man of all his labour which he taketh under the sun?
>
> One generation passeth away, and another generation cometh; but the earth abideth for ever.
>
> The sun also ariseth, and the sun also goeth down, and haseth to his place where he arose.

All things belonging to this world are mere vanity, in fact, vanity of vanities. People go on toiling all through their lives, but they hardly get anything out of what they do. No doubt, people come and go; the sun appears and disappears; the wind blows to and fro; everything is perishable, and yet, says the Preacher, the earth abides for ever. There is a good deal of frustration and perversion and disenchantment in *The Sun Also Rises*; the whole climate, the very atmosphere of this novel is dominated by excessive drinking, meaningless holidaying and promiscuity, and yet the picture of the Irati riverside and that of the carefree and dancing Basque people make us believe that all is not yet over; that there is still some room for hope, and that in spite of all infection and sickness and morbidity the earth will abide for ever. In this context we have to take special note of the way Hemingway describes the gaiety of the Basque peasants, raw and vigorous and virile in *The Sun Also Rises* :

> People were coming into the square from all sides, and down the street we heard the pipes and the fifes and the drums coming. They were playing the *riau-riau* music, the pipes shrill and the drums pounding, and behind them came the men and boys dancing. When the fifers stopped they all crouched down in the street, and when the reed-pipes and the fifes shrilled, and the flat, dry hollow drums tapped it out again, they all went up in the air dancing.

> In the crowd you saw only the heads and shoulders of the dancers going up and down (118).

The psychological, the spiritual darkness is there; Hemingway makes use of the word 'dark' (119) several times in the novel in both its physical and spiritual sense, and still he describes the 'sun' (159) as an object, a symbol of light and life, as a force or phenomenon that makes everything 'bright' (159) and 'radiant' (159).

## IV

Considered as a novel, *The Sun Also Rises* may seem to be 'a slight thing' (Wagenknecht, 369); at times it may even be dismissed as 'an immoral book' (Wagenknecht, 375) chiefly for the reason that the world of this novel is a world of drunken promiscuity, and yet we cannot and should not lose sight of the fact that Hemingway did have his own interest in the problem of the meaning and values of human life, that his is 'an intensely implicational' (Wagenknecht, 372) mode of writing in spite of his austere and sparse style, that he 'rarely interprets his juxtapositions for us' (Wagenknecht, 372), that his novels do contain 'submerged' (Hemphill 50-60) meanings, and that his images do function as the 'symbols of an inner world' (Cowley 316-17). Mark Spilka says the very same thing in a different way when he states that 'with Hemingway, the great outdoors is chiefly a state of mind, a projection of moral and emotional attitudes on to physical arenas, so that a clear account of surface action will reproduce these attitudes in the reader' (Shapiro 245).

As we have said earlier, it is for quite understandable reasons that we find images of emptiness in *The Sun Also Rises*, but it is also equally understandable that these images of emptiness are generally followed by those of cleansing, mopping up or sweeping. Similarly, quite a few of the other images that we get in the present novel relate chiefly to the false knight, Robert Cohn, though there are some that take us straight on to the bull-fighter, Pedro Romero. In the preceding pages we have also discussed at some length the importance of such images as present to us an integrated picture of happiness, growth and fruitfulness amidst despair, decay and degeneration. It is in this very light that we have to interpret the goat image and the images pertaining to bull-fight and fishing.

At this point it is important to refer to the suggestiveness of some of the symbols — the symbol of rain, the symbol of the game of poker dice, the symbol of a mounted policeman directing traffic, the symbol of Brett Ashley's trembling hands and the symbol of the scars of arrow wounds on the Count's back in particular — that we get in *The Sun Also Rises*. We have also considered the present novel as a parable; as an extended parable in fact, in which images and symbols do have their own value, and we have as well tried to bring out the allegorical significance of the title of this novel, which has been taken from *Ecclesiastes* of the *Old Testament* and which suggests that though all is vanity, vanity of vanities really, the earth abides for ever.

It is sometimes contended that since Hemingway was concerned chiefly with the representation of 'the real thing' (*D.A.* 6) and wanted to state the whole thing in a direct and straightforward manner, there is hardly any room for the intentional use of symbols in his novels. And though to a certain extent this attitude may be correct, yet we do come across images and symbols in his writings. However, there are two things that have to be taken note of in this connection. The first is that Hemingway makes use of his symbols so skilfully and so unobtrusively that they do not seem to have been used at all. And, secondly, most of the symbols in his novels are used in the form of images; his images do have their own symbolic value, and it is indeed very difficult to draw a line of distinction between his images and his symbols.

## WORKS CITED

Cowley, Malcolm, Introduction. *Ernest Hemingway : The Man and His Work.* New York : n.p., 1944.

Farrell, James, *The League of Frightened Philistines.* New York : n.p., 1945.

Hemingway, Ernest, *Death in the Afternoon.* n.p., Penguin Books, 1966.

——, *The Sun Also Rises.* n.p., Penguin edition, 1974.

Hemphill, George, "Hemingway and James". *Kenyon Review* XI, 1949.

Philip Young, *Ernest Hemingwary.* New York, 1952.

Shapiro, Charles, ed., *Twelve Original Essays on Great American Novels.* Detroit : n.p., 1958.

Wagenknecht, E., *Cavalcade of the American Novels.* Calcutta : n.p., 1952.

# 10

# They are not Meant for Defeat : An Appraisal of the Hemingway Heroes in *A Farewell to Arms*, *For Whom the Bell Tolls* and *The Old Man and the Sea*

*—Amiya Kumar Patra*

## I

AS A novelist Ernest Miller Hemingway (1899-1961) aims at making his protagonists the winners in the game of life. He is concerned with the theme of suffering and endurance of his characters and crowns them with abstract prizes. They are not, declares Hemingway, "meant for defeat" (1952 : 103). Underscoring this point of view critics like Carlos Baker, Philip Young, Stewart Sanderson, Earl Rovit and Leslie Fielder portray Hemingway's hero as the outdoor male who faces his destiny with a super human effort. But not much attention has been given to the protagonist's entrapment in the course of the journey towards his own destiny. Of course, we find a hint of it in Milton Howard. He is of the opinion that Hemingway heroes are sometimes called "helpless victims of forces — cosmic, social, physical, psychological — over which they have no control, men without free will, without the power to control their own destiny" (1952 : 05). I would like to take cue from this statement in farming the nucleus of the present study. Howard's stand, as the ensuing analysis would attempt to establish, is not wholly acceptable. For Hemingway's hero is an all time winner though destroyed badly in the process of winning. Again, Howard does not elaborate upon the idea of victimization. He is also not emphatic in portraying the victimized protagonist who turns out to be a real winner.

A cursory reading of the texts of Hemingway's major novels may miss the fact that though often victims, in a mundane sense, Hemingway heroes invariably, snatch away victory from the jaws of defeat by their sheer determination and understanding of life. All of them, though pure losers in a material sense, are real winners on a metaphysical plane. Frederick Henry in *A Farewell to Arms* (1929) is a victim of fate, a loser both in war and love. But after receiving the scars of life he learns to live with them gracefully. Robert Jordan in *For Whom The Bell Tolls* (1940) realizes that something can be done before the end and with the realization he grasps the code and waits for something to die for. Santiago in *The Old Man and the Sea* (1953) returns with the skeleton of his trophy. Nevertheless, he achieves dignity by putting up a brave fight to the end. Although much has been said about the heroism of these protagonists Hemingway studies so far have not adequately treated them as winners in relation to their victimization. This study attempts at analysing the various forces as well as the process of victimization of Hemingway heroes and seeks to highlight their eventual emergence as winners.

Critics broadly divide Hemingway's major characters into two categories : the 'Hemingway hero' and the 'code hero.' Earl Rovit calls them the 'tyro' and the 'tutor' respectively. Hemingway hero (tyro) is a young man (or a young boy) who learns to live in the world where there, is chaos, violence, uncertainty and anxiety. He learns by receiving wounds and by being victimized. The code hero, (tutor) on the contrary, is usually an older person who has become what he had to become. He has realized his potentialities and has known the area of his operation. He is usually a Professional — a bull-fighter, a fisherman, a veteran soldier or a prize fighter. He is sure to excel in his pursuit and he does not step out of that before the end. He possesses, as the code prescribes, immense resources of courage and endurance which will enable him, despite all pressures, to confront destruction and death with boldness and dignity. He is the symbol of the fighting spirit of man. Both 'Hemingway hero' and the 'code hero' are destroyed or mangled in the course of the gratification of their passion — physical or social or spiritual. All of them are subject to the same process of victimization culminating in graceful victory. When we meet them bearing the scars of life, it is possible to gauge the degree of their victimization and the height of dignity, with which they bore it.

The genesis of 'Hemingway hero' lies in Nick Adams who first appears in the author's collection of short stories, *In Our Times* (1952). When Nick attains manhood he is introduced to the violence and evils of the world. As a result, he is wounded and crippled both physically and psychologically and ultimately falls out with society. Philip Young in *Hemingway : A Reconsideration* remarks :

> It is important to understand this Nick, for soon, under other names in other books, he is going to be known half the world over as the "Hemingway hero" every single one of these men has had, or has had the exact equivalent of, Nick's childhood, adolescence; and young manhood. This man will die a thousand times before his death, and although he would learn how to live with some of his troubles, and how to overcome others, he would never completely recover from his wounds as long as Hemingway lived and recorded his adventures (1966 : 1971).

Hemingway's Protagonists are essentially wounded both physically and psychologically. There is no healing for this wound. Yet he bears the pain and lives and lasts stoically. "The Hemingway hero", comments Stewart Sanderson, by whatever name he appears, carries both physical and psychic scars. Hemingway's basic preoccupations is how to live with these scars" (1961 : 32).

In *The Sun Also Rises* (1926) Jake Barnes is a less personal hero than Nick. But he is the same man, a grown Nick Adams, and again the actual injury functions as concrete evidence that the hero is a causality. Jake like Nick is broken with society. Jake in order to, live up to his code, complains very little although psychologically he suffers a great deal. He is sick at heart. He is troubled by the war, by old grievances. He knows he has little use for his friends, for society, even for himself. He works as a newspaper reporter just to make enough money to drink, eat and spend most of the time in the cafés, or in fishing or in watching bull-fights.

*A Farewell to Arms* (1929) can be read as a companion piece to the earlier novel. Some of Brett's past is filled in by Catherine Barkley, whose finance had been blown to pieces by the war. And in certain ways Fredrick Henry complements Jake Barnes. Here the protagonist is victimized twice — first in the arms of war and then in the arms of love. The Hemingway hero suffers defeat but suffers it gallantly. The novel ends with Catherine's death in a caesarean operation. Bereft of his partner, his last refuge from the cruelties of life, Henry reaches a tragic height by remaining undaunted at the moment of destruction. He, therefore, achieves a moral victory though destroyed in war and love.

In Hemingway's next novel *To Have and Have Not* (1937) we find a great difference between the man chasing animals in Africa and the protagonist of this novel. The protagonist, Hary Morgan, finds it impossible to make an honest living for himself. He is victimized by poverty. If he can neither govern nor control his own life in a chosen way, he has to learn to live with reality and chance. He does exactly the same. Hence the absolvement of his victim-hood.

In 1940 appears *For Whom the Bell Tolls*, one of the most significant novels of Hemingway. The protagonist Robert Jordan is a participant in the Spanish Civil War. He is politically committed and therefore becomes a victim of his commitment. He struggles between his wish to live and his old obsession with death. At the end Robert dies but before that he grasps the code; he finds something to die for. Therefore, a winner in the moral plane.

As a tribute to the fighting spirit of man, *The Old Man and the Sea* appears in 1952. Here Hemingway is concerned with life's struggle against insurmountable odds. Here the protagonist has to pay for going far out into the sea, for aspiring to be more than the common lot. The victim, the Old man, fails to bring the prize he wins back to the shore. Sharks eat away the marlin. The Old man, the fisherman par excellence, takes nothing except the satisfaction that he has tried his best. He bears the loss boldly without feeling that he has lost. His courage and endurance raise him to the level of Hemingway's code and he attains moral triumph thereby.

In the course of this study I propose to analyze Hemingway's three such novels as *A Farewell to Arms*, *For Whom the Bells Tolls* and *The Old Man and the Sea* where victimization of the protagonists is not pronounced, and, what is more the protagonists' ultimate victory has not been recognized, let alone celebrated, by Hemingway critics. As these protagonists, by whatever name they appear, carry both physical and psychological scars and mostly meet their end tragically critics tend to treat them as failures. This study, however, aims at bestowing upon these victims the status of winners which they rightly deserve.

## II

Courage, endurance and love, Hemingway asserts emphatically in his writings, are the only sustaining factors in a world where man is, invariably, destined to be trapped and broken, where life can only end badly. Fredrick Henry, Hemingway's protagonist in *A Farewell to Arms* bears out this message fully in his own life which is a tale of spiritual victory through victimization by agents : social, political and providential as well.

Like Hemingway's other protagonists Fredrick Henry also emerges out of his harrowing war time experiences. He is one of Hemingway's alter egos who embodies some of his most private desires. It is at the front that Hemingway gets to know the harsh world that wants to solve all conflicts by war; a world of wolves where everyone wars on everyone else. The years following the first World War witnesses the revolt, the breaking away and the partial return to the parental home of the so-called 'lost generation.' The War makes Hemingway see death without disguise or heroic illusion and gazing at its grim face he begins to treat organized death as a social phenomenon inherent in a world that surrounds him. Crippled and frustrated by their war time experiences, depressed by the fear of coming crises people fall victims to the social disease of the age. Tired and empty hearted they are hunted by the end of hope. Hemingway as a literary artist comes nearest to the decadent philosophy of his time through his wounded characters. But characters like Henry in *A Farewell to Arms* who represent the 'Lost Generation' are not lost. They have seen the light at the end of the tunnel. Although losers in the game of life they have not submitted to its preposterous ways. They stand like lone Promotheuses and provide the possibility of an alternative existence to the otherwise grim one they have lived through.

*A Farewell to Arms* is first published in 1929 and instantly marks Hemingway's most distinctive development as a literary artist. The axis of the novel, considered from the point of view of the development of the hero-figure, is to be found in the sixth inter-story of *In Our Times*, where we find that Nick Adams, hit in the spine is waiting for the stretcher-bearers to come. Another story under the title "A Very Short Story" supplies the other axis, for here we are introduced to the love affair between a wounded soldier and a nurse in a military hospital.

Two themes namely, the theme of war and the theme of love dominate the plot of this fiction. But they are never narrated separately. Both the themes are intermingled. In the first part of the novel we are introduced to the war and the lovers whom it brings together. Love and war go side by side with Frederick Henry till the end. Much before the end of the story Henry rejects war. But war never releases him from its clutches. While Henry rejects war for love, love is to come to an end soon with the death of Catherine. Henry is victimized twice : first in the war and then in love.

War, writes B.K. Tripathy, is a "right spanking monster and easily lends itself as a victimizer. It has the army, the labyrinthine war fields, and the barracks for the incarceration of the victim (1985 : 186)." In *A Farewell to Arms* it presents a closed society which makes more rigorous the entrapment of individuals in it. The novel opens with an immobile army unit. The locale is Northern Italy during the First World War. A Company of Italian army is being introduced to us with real characters. There is disillusioned Rinaldi, the Italian army surgeon, happy with his profession, wine and sex. This man, apparently having no values, is god at heart. Ettore Moretti is a boastful young Californian whose sole ambition is promotion. There are other like Bonello, Passini, Aymo, all with the feeling of entrapment, waiting to be freed. There is also Gordini, the Ambulance head, who is much more interested in the welfare of his lieutenant rather than himself. But mostly we develop our acquaintance with Frederick Henry, the young American lieutenant in the Ambulance corps. "Rootless, haunted by a lack of purpose, deadened by his own escapist cynicism, searching for something to sustain his spirit, he is entrapped by war (*ibidem* : 18)." Our next concern is Catherine Barkley, the priestly, calm and selfless English V.A.D. nurse, who with the development of the plot keeps Henry's spirits buoyant and alive.

Henry is a perfectly normal young man, a real Yankee. He is rather selfish, rather casual about the suffering of others, somewhat indifferent to the consequences of his actions, wilfully a victim of his own self-indulgence. He is only a tourist through life and war. His entrapment in war involves a period of wandering in the wilderness from which escape seems impossible. Henry is a party boy who is motivated by an ill defined idealism and a vague romantic urge to join the peace corps. He wears his officer's uniform with a casual pride. His initial concern is drinking and wenching. Henry's situation at the beginning of the novel is very much like an American teen-age male's dream of overseas duty.

As we move on through the novel we are made to recognize the fact that it is not a war story or a love story so much as it is a modern morality drama — the dramatization of the developing consciousness of a young American in the twentieth century context of war. Henry's growth as an individual being is a very painful one. His fortified self is shaken and callousness moved when he is initiated into love by the Priest. Catherine acts as a guardian angel whose presence metamorphoses the self-centered adventure seeker into the lover prepared to forgo his self for the sake of the beloved. Of course, there are Rinaldi and Passini who boost his moral growth. Finally it is the personal physical wound, the first hand experience of the sufferings of war, and a kind of consummation with death inside the ambulance which prepare the ground for the separate peace he is to make and from this point on he is on his way to freedom from the victim-hood of war. We would do well here to draw a brief sketch of Henry's progress from a hollow other directed man to a sensitized being thoroughly purged in the fire of suffering.

From within the prison of the self Henry is unable to interact with the external world. But he is able to take himself rather seriously when the priest asks Henry whether he loves God, he replies "No" and it boils down to "I do not love much" (Hemingway 1929 : 37). Then the priest defines love. It is not what Henry does on leave in the centers of "Culture and Civilization." It is rather manifested in service and sacrifice for the beloved one. "When you love you wish to do thing for. You wish to sacrifice for. You wish to serve" (*ibidem* : 57). The Priest prescribes a commitment beyond oneself, beyond the unattached condition and attitude of Henry at this point in the novel, a commitment he would achieve later with the English nurse, Catherine Barkley.

For the present, love to Henry is but a sub-game, a role defined by the larger game of war. Love for him is a "game like bridge in which you said things instead of playing cards (*ibidem* : 27)." The emptiness within Henry resembles the absurd world without. Nothing at this point has meaning or connects the inside with the outside except immediate physical sensation. This is why Henry prefers to insulate himself in sensations rather than going to the cold, clear and, dry mountains of Abruzzi where the Priest's home is.

It is Rinaldi who informs Henry about the lovely British V.A.D. nurse. But he takes it casually and prefers to talk about the girls at the Villa Rosa. Again, when Rinaldi introduces Henry to Catherine Barkley, the nurse, Henry merely regards her as a sexual prospect. When Catherine asks him, "Have you ever loved any one?", he could give an unequivocal "No" (*ibidem* : 18).

Even after Henry is wounded the reality of war does not penetrate his consciousness. As observed by the Priest, it is just an impersonal accident for him. "Still even wounded," the Priest says on his visit to the field hospital, "you do not see it, I can tell" (*ibidem* : 55). What Henry obviously does not see is that war is a destroyer of love through its fundamental irrational violence, that war is a destroyer of individual through its obliteration of individual dignity and importance. We see that even Henry's perfunctory commitment to the war has robbed him of both his capacity to act and react as an individual. He fails to perceive unlike Passini, the ambulance driver, and the Priest that war as a game is absurd, that there is nothing important in winning or losing, that it believes only in destruction and recognizes no side. The forces of victimization in war are so strong that Henry is drawn to it in a natural way. He goes on trying to make war meaningful within the chaos and absurdities of the retreat until the incident at the bridge removes his blindness. He begins to be afflicted by the horrible and dehumanizing results of war. Throughout the war-dominated portions of the novel we observe Henry's growing frustration in attempting to assess the 'incomprehensibility' of 'madness' acted out on a mass scale. This madness is so far-reaching in its scope that it is beyond the grasp of the individual caught up, as he is, in the web. "Perhaps wars weren't won any more : the truth crystallizes slowly : May be they go on forever (*ibidem* : 117).

The mortar attack in the front marks Henry's discovery of the victim experience in war. This is a vital landmark in the progress of Henry's character. The experience of death makes his moral resurrection possible. The mortar attack which leaves him almost dead makes him see with Passini and the Priest that there is nothing worse than war. His illusions about war dissolves. As he is brought into the field hospital in an ambulance, the soldier in the stretcher above begins to bleed and the steady flow of blood drenches Henry.

> "The steam kept on. In the dark I could not see where it came from the canvas overhead.... I tried to move sideways so that it did not fall on me...it made me sick...and started drip again and I heard and felt the canvas above move as the man on the stretcher settled more comfortably" (*ibidem* : 49).

In Henry's experience of agony and death one discerns a kind of a ritual which makes his resurrection possible. Passini, his compatriot, dies at his side. The death is at once followed by a ritual baptism in blood of an unknown solider. There inside the womb of the van Henry establishes a conscious inter-personal bond. He is enlarged. The play-boy, is initiated into a fresh awareness through inter-personal relationship.

Henry is wounded and a real awareness of war thus comes about with the shock of physical sensation. The next step in the process of his awareness involves a fuller realization of what war can do to others. Henry's period of staying at the American Hospital in Milan is primarily the story of his increasing attachment with Catherine Barkley. His connection with war is rather tenuously established through the newspapers and one or two conversations with other soldiers.

Henry's disillusionment with war is yet reinforced by his reunion with Rinaldi. Rinaldi doubts that he has syphilis and suspects everyone is trying to get rid of him. He has been pushed to the edge. The baiting by the young men at the mess used to make him blush. But that does not affect him any more. He is no longer a believer in victory, rather in his heart of hearts he wishes that the war should stop. This is an expression of the desperate hope of a tried young man who has realized the evils of war. Henry adds to the discouragement of the Priest by suggesting that it is in defeat that man knows what war is, since the Austrians have won by beating back the advance they will not stop fighting. "What do you believe in?" asks the Priest. "In sleep," he replies. There has been a change somewhere in Henry's thinking. He no more believes in victory or defeat. So when he says "sleep" he means something more than that — he is physically tired. He is tired of war. It may mean that he sees at last that in the war everyone loses and the goal he has set before him is really empty. There is no doubt that without the incident at the bridge or one like it Henry would have continued to serve until the end of the war or the end of himself.

Here at this turning point of the novel where Henry is made capable of bidding farewell to arms Hemingway extends the absurdity of war to the absurd existence of Man. Like the war, the world "kills the very good and the very gentle and the very brave impartially (*ibidem* : 153)" and without reason. Once born and involved in the process of living, one, Henry is made to realize, cannot wriggle out of it without bearing scars or getting killed.

> That was what you did. You died, you did not know what it was about. You never had time to learn. They threw you in and told you the rules and the first time they caught you off base they killed you. Or they killed you gratuitously like Aymo or gave you the syphilis like Rinaldi. But they killed you in the end. You could count on that. Stay around and they would kill you (*ibidem* : 232).

This rather caustic observation on life is acted out by the harsh parable of the ants steamed to death on the log of a camp fire.

The world kills or at the least, as a rule, breaks everyone. Yet some, broken and maimed, learn another set of rules to survive with dignity. Henry, as we shall presently discuss, learns the rules of a victorious survivor as his relationship with Catherine, intensifies into love. In their first meeting Henry takes her to be a play thing. In the second meeting he is slapped by her for attempting to force a kiss. But he is happy on account of her aggressive stance. After all, she is not an available girl. In their next meeting Henry takes Catherine to be a "little crazy" due to the death of her young fiancé, the one she had deeply loved, in the war. While she is in love, Henry shows a different attitude. "I know," tells Henry, "I did not love Catherine Barkley nor had any idea of loving her (*ibidem* : 27)." Love for him is like a game of bridge where instead of playing cards "you said things." Catherine being fully aware of this attitude declares the game to be a rotten one. She does not need to be told that she is loved by Henry : You do not have to say you love me. That's all over for a while (*ibidem* : 27).

Love is resumed again in Milan hospital where it no longer remains a game. Henry feels "lonely and hollow" in her absence. This is not simply an acknowledgement of love. It is a human awakening to the need for a relationship that goes beyond the physical. The Byronic hero is at the threshold of a new experience. As soon as he sees Catherine coming through the door he knows that he is in love with her. Their relationship is no longer a matter of empty words, of calculated moves towards the checkmate of seduction. He wishes to marry Catherine. She sees no need in this : "We are married privately. You see, darling, it would mean everything to me if I would have any religion. But I have not any religion" (*ibidem* : 85). Catherine's refusal of marriage is a refusal of God and religion.

This refusal might also be a result of her desire to save him from a sense of burden. She would rather sacrifice all her interest to see him happy. "There isn't any me any more" I want what you want" (*ibidem* : 79). Thus the Priest's definition of love is worked out for and brought home to Henry by Catherine. Love makes it easier and quicker for him to get released from the victimization of the war and the world as well.

Before returning to the front Henry is momentarily disturbed about Catherine's pregnancy. His decision, not withstanding the feeling of being biologically trapped, to have the child saves him from another instance of losing out to war, the victimizer. Along side the war Henry's internal journey proceeds on.

At the front defeat stares the Italians on the face. During the retreat from, Caporetto Henry is arrested by the battle police, suspected of being a German in Italian uniform. He who has stubbornly refused to desert is taken to be a deserter. At once, he realizes that the monster of war is one. It knows no side, no patriotism. Once trapped in it, whichever way one turns the same *Minotaur* pursues. With this realization he jumps into the flooded Tagliamento from the bridge and swims across thc line of fire to safety. "Anger was washed away in the river along with any obligation" (*ibidem* : 167). In a symbolic gesture he throws away his uniform as hail of bullets come after him. He establishes his separate peace. A conscious rejection of war now makes him free, free from the clutches of the *Minotaur*, to render his love Catherine complete.

Henry and Catherine have to flee Tressa to Switzerland. There she grows big with the child. Her labour begins with the beginning of spring rain. At Lausanne hospital her condition deteriorates. Caesarian operation is done but the child is still born. Catherine has to succumb to a dirty trick played on her. Henry is desperate seeing her, his last refuge, dying before him. There '*nada*' stares him on face. He prays for her life;

> Don't let her die. Oh, God, don't. Please, please, dear God. Don't let her die. I will do anything for you if you won't let her die. Please, please, please, dear God, don't let her die....You took the baby but don't let her die (*ibidem* : 234).

But no prayer is ever answered in Hemingway's world. The bribe, the sacrificial offering of the baby in exchange of Catherine's life goes in vain.

With Catherine's death Henry is all the more exposed than ever before to the absurds proposition that life, war being only a fragmentary manifestation of it, is. He is caught whichever way he turns. For him the death of his love is yet another "unreasonable wound", an arbitrary happening in a mindless universe. Catherine's death proves victimization to be a part of the game and entrapment inevitable. Surely Henry has been a victim of War because of his own blindness and because of the greater impersonal forces that War represents. First the mortar attack, the blood bath, and, then Catherine's love apparently liberates him from his victim-hood. He deserts the army to take refuge in love. Yet he is not out of the pattern of victimization. He is trapped in love. "He is trapped biologically," observes Philip Young, "that costs him his future wife in the harrowing scenes at the hospital..." (1959, 1964 : 93). The unreasonable wound talked about in the parable of ants is enacted in a great magnitude in his own life. He flees war only to be wounded permanently in love. Thus Henry's unreasonable wounds quite reasonably make him a victim of fate, of life. Nonetheless his courage, and, endurance, and, most important of all, his insight into life offer him the status of a winner.

As the novel closes Henry walks away from the hotel in rain. His losses are too heavy for words or for tears. Stewart Sanderson in *Hemingway* remarks : "The Hemingway hero, by whatever name he, appears, carries both, physical and psychic scars. Hemingway's basic preoccupation is how to live with these scars" (1961 : 32). All that Henry can do with dignity is to maintain a stiff upper lip, endure his pain quietly without crying, and remain alive. It is in the struggles of living he defeats defeat and denies the denials of life. He is destroyed in the process of victimization but bears the sears with pride. Gracefully bearing the marks of suffering he rises to the height of the 'Code Hero.' He comes to learn that the ultimate reality is death and the world breaks everyone and what one has to do in order to live is "to remain strong at the broken places." With this wisdom Henry the victim of the life qualifies to be a true winner in living.

### III

If in *A Farewell to Arms* Henry falls a victim to his callousness, ignorance, and, then to the monster of war and still later to an absurd human existence in *For Whom the Bell Tolls* (1940) Robert Jordan is a victim of his political commitment. His love for Spain turns to be his ruling passion, and his objective to save Spain his obsession. The process of his entrapment and victimization emanates from this commitment which obliterates such other vital considerations as personal will, political ideology and love. Presently we shall see how, through the course of his victimization, Jordan grasps the Hemingway code and thereby gets released from his self-inflicted victim-hood and emerges a winner, through courage, endurance, love, and, faith in achieving something before the end.

*For Whom the Bell Tolls*, Hemingway's most directly political and to a great extent autobiographical novel, is situated in the Civil War torn Spain which Hemingway visited as a war correspondent and about which he wrote a play entitled *The Fifth Column*. In writing *For Whom the Bell Tolls* and developing its characters Hemingway again applies the technique of novelizing personal experience. Many of his friends appear in the novel, sometimes under their actual names and sometimes in 'thin disguise.' Duran, the Loyalist commander, and, Petra, Hemingway's chamber maid at Hotel Florida appear by name. The Polish General Karol is portrayed under the disguise of General Golz. Koltsov, the journalist bears the fictional name of Karokov. Maria is a "Superb blending of two women", one is a nurse whom Hemingway met in Mafaro and the other is Martha Gellhorn, his third wife. The nurse contributes to the spiritual part of Maria. Jordan, the Protagonist, at best shares many of the personal characteristics and opinions of his creator. Hemingway even gives Jordan one of his most prominent traits — a red, black, killing anger.

Robert Jordan is a thin and tall young man with "sun-stretched fair hair, and a wind and sum-burned face" (Hemingway 1940 : 67). Originally an instructor in Spanish in a small college in America he comes to spend his vacations in Spain with a view to improve his Spanish. He never feels like a foreigner in Spain and his love for and loyalty to the republic is absolute and almost borders on fanaticism. When the civil war breaks out he fights for the republic as an American volunteer in order to contribute his best towards the welfare of Spain. He knows that whatever be the outcome of the war, he would like to see that what he loves in Spain is preserved. He is reluctant to give himself a political label except that of an anti-Fascist because his convictions are so different from those of the Russians who are conducting the war for the Republicans. Still he is committed to the political cause of the country. Jordan's love for Spain is so overpowering that against his desire to be labeled politically, he is committed politically. In gratification of this passion he falls prey to it and becomes a victim of his own political commitment. We need to keep this in mind from the beginning that if this commitment is the source of Jordan's victimization his path to victory also lies in suffering it out courageously with a positive attitude. He is a victim of his commitment because, good or bad, he is determined to accomplish the duty — blowing up the bridge — assigned to him. He is further vulnerable to victimization because of his obsession with violence and death. All for his talks about social justice for the people of Spain he loves, his zeal to destroy the Fascists smacks of a denial of life. Still victory is assured for him when love comes to his rescue and he starts reasserting life. But he won't swerve away from his commitment. He makes the most of his last hours and accepts death with courage and stoic endurance as Jake does in *The Sun Also Rises*.

Jordan's primary concern is war and how to win over it. If he fails in the pursuit everything is lost. He "gave absolute loyalty and as complete performance as he could give while he was serving" (*ibidem* : 132). He is committed to fight for the 'liberty', 'dignity' and rights for all men to work and not to be hungry. Karkov, the Russian Journalist, thinks that Jordan's political education is meager but the Russian General Golz thinks very highly of him as a 'partisan' dynamiter and therefore gives him the most difficult assignment :

> "Merely to blow the bridge is a failure."
> "Yes Comrade General."
> "To blow the bridge at a stated hour based on time set for the attack is how it should be done.
> That is your right and how it should be done" (*ibidem* : 8).

Jordan's absolute commitment to this tough assignment entraps him in the process of its execution. The uncertainty of the job makes it tougher and further hardens the course of his victimization. Jordan is expected to work with strangers and rely on them for the success of his assignment. There is no certainty of the time to blow up the bridge or whether it would be required at all. In a whirlpool of uncertainty Jordan stands for certainty when he says with confidence, "It will start on time..." (*ibidem* : 9). He is ready to take up any risk to justify the faith of General Golz on him. The ritual of victimization commences when Jordan finally asks to know what sort of uniform he is supposed to wear. He is already too motivated to resist the process of victimization which comes in the form of his commitment. There is yet another side, though not much different from to his political commitment : his commitment relating to Maria who for him symbolizes Spain and her sufferings. The memory of his grandfather's valor infuses him with the strength and courage to fight and achieve what he wishes to achieve. The invocation is magical in keeping his fighting spirit on and at the same time dragging Jordan farther towards victimization and destruction.

On closer examination we find that Jordan's commitment to the Spanish cause may not be as pure as it appears to be. Perhaps it is greatly motivated by his personal anger and a desire to wash of the painful memory of his father's shameful suicide. Hence his constant recollection of his grandfather, "a hell of a good soldier", and his disappointment when the attack is postponed. We have enough reason to suspect that in the beginning Jordan is pushed forward in his commitment by a craze to achieve personal glory. This may explain the austerity of his devotion to violence, sanctified and made morally palatable by the orders he receives as a dynamiter. Both Pablo and Anselmo may be reluctant figures but their reluctance strikes a positive note. Pablo has grown weary of the continued butchery and Anselmo is deeply aware of the horror involved in taking human life. Although Pablo still fights for the loyalty cause, his ultimate commitment is to be survival of himself and his people. Jordan on the other hand looks upon the war itself as a kind of climax to his commitment and his commitment an end in itself. Such an attitude makes Jordan an easy victim of war and his passion to give his best to it. While it is time that his love for Maria steers the course of his life toward victory it was not so in the beginning. Maria's violation by the Fascists only intensifies his passion to prove his mettle in the war. It is only later on that Jordan feels inseparable from Maria who becomes all woman for him and begins to dream of a future life with her. The sources of Jordan's victimization and victory are the same; only the attitude decides whither he must turn.

The victim as we see always concentrates on job. Jordan is devoted so much so to his voluntary service that he turns to be a sort of a masochist. "He was serving in war and he gave absolute loyalty and as complete performance as he could give while he was serving" (*ibidem* : 132). This statement declares the stranglehold of victimization on the protagonist. The grip is further tightened when he says to himself, "Spain was your work and your job…so the demolition was a second and normal job too" (*ibidem* : 160). The protagonist is so much job oriented that he is ready to follow orders without any judgment : "You follow orders. Follow them and don't try to think beyond them" (*ibidem* : 316). Thus any escape for him from the clutch of victimization is a remote possibility until and unless he is destroyed in the process.

Love as a rule, has no place in the course of victimization. Yet, the fact remains that Jordan's relationship with Maria matures into love and it guarantees his emancipation from victim-hood. But, again, in the love also victory and victimization overlaps. It is victory when love fulfils his life and helps overcome all the odds of his political commitment. It is victimization when the cause of Maria tightens still harder the noose of death and destruction round his neck. And, of course, ultimately victory overweighs.

Maria, Jordan's "my woman",. with her cropped hair like "the golden brown" of a green field (*ibidem* : 25) becomes the symbol of Spain for him. He receives so much from her that he is easily disturbed if anything troubles her. So he gets infuriated when she says that she does not knows how to kiss but things were done to her by the Fascists. He receives another blow when Maria tells him. That her barrenness is due to the mass rape by the Fascists. On a personal level Jordan finds this blow to be unbearable.... He feels duty bound to take revenge and let loose violence. His love for Maria and his task of blowing up the bridge become one. He has to blow up the bridge for the Russian General as well as for the Republic which has been raped, like Maria, by the Fascist. Fighting for the Republic becomes more compulsive because in his mind the Republic and Maria become one. It is this compulsion that makes him lie on the pine-needle-covered floor at the end of the novel waiting for the Fascist Lieutenant and thus helping Pablo and his band to retreat into the Gredos hills. His loyalty to the Republic becomes a personal issue and his action that of a husband covering the retreat of the wife he loves. Though this self-oriented urge to set things right contribute largely to his mental victimization, his ultimate extension of the self to selfless loving desire to sacrifice — "You can do nothing for yourself but perhaps you can do something for another" (*ibidem* : 443) — frees him from victimhood.

As already hinted, Jordan's love for Maria not only propels him on the path of violence and destruction it also brings him back to life. Maria's love comes like a soft, soothing dream into the life of this victimized being. He wonders :

> Such things do not happen. May be it never did happen, he thought. May be you dreamed it or made it up and

> never did happen. May be it is like the dreams you have when some one you have seen in the cinema comes to your bed at night and is so kind and lovely.... May be it was like those dreams (*ibidem* : 333).

Dreams are to be dissolved soon and Maria is to vanish from Jordan's life. But thanks to her, his attitude towards life undergoes a wholesome change. For this disillusioned soldier Maria becomes all women with whom he could ever have any relationship, his sister, wife and daughter. "I never had a true, love. I never had a wife. She is also my sister, and my daughter, and I never will have a daughter. I have to leave a thing that is so good" (*ibidem* : 360).

Pilar, the strongest ally of Jordan, is a forty-eight-year old gypsy woman who plays the key role in bringing Jordan and Maria together. She is a half-witch and half woman who reads death in Jordan's palm. She also knows that he is obsessed with death and thus is becoming impotent and cannot complete the 'task' so important for the victory of the Republic. Like a mother she wishes to sustain the spirit of Jordan with the love of Maria. Having seen that Maria is attracted to the young American dynamiter Pilar literally pushes her into his sleeping bag for two reasons : if Jordan remains alive after his mission Maria would go with him to lead a normal life; Maria's love would make up for what he has suffered in case he gets killed. Pilar sincerely wishes that love would relieve Jordan from the tension his mission creates in him and also recover Maria from the shock she has received because of rape and the death of her parents by the Fascists. Pilar's wishes are fulfilled. Love enables Jordan turn from death to life. Within the very brief span of the narration he makes love to Maria five times and each time he is relieved of his tension and worries. Love also helps him get rid of his bigotry. Maria's love comes to him in the challenging hours of his life. Now on he is capable of looking forward to life, to survival, to a happy married life with Maria as "Mr. and Mrs. Robert Jordan of Sun Valley, Idaho." Love, of course, is to disappear soon but not before leaving him fulfilled. Love is that alchemy which turns the victim to a victor. Destruction may very well be his destiny but it is compensated by the relishing taste of victory.

The end comes swiftly. Jordan follows the orders and succeeds in destroying the bridge though the losses are too heavy, and, much beyond his anticipation. He is very badly wounded and death is certain for him. Yet he brings all the difference to it, which would have been otherwise, a victimization, by his graceful acceptance of it. Death, he asks, where is they sting? And he wins over death by yielding to it not as a man committed to death and destruction but as one committed to life and love. He has lived a full life of seventy years in just seventy hours. At the hour of death Jordan's love for Maria and the Republic is complete. His faith in the sustaining force of love is rendered all the more unshakable with the knowledge, that he is to bid adieu to life soon. So he does not die in death as he shares : his life with and goes on to live in Maria : "Thou wilt go, rabbit. But I go with thee. As long as there is one of us there is both of us" (*ibidem* : 436).

Jordan gracefully endures his physical pain which is beyond common human endurance. He is without regret or despair. While waiting to kill Lieutenant Berrendo and for death he lies content on he brown pine needle floor of the forest that at last he is going to live in Maria and in the republic; that he has found a real cause to die for. Perhaps there could not be a more glorious death and only a victor and a victor alone deserves it.

## IV

Of the two categories of Hemingway protagonists : (1) Tyro (hero) and (2) Tutor (Code hero) Santiago belongs to the second one and as such has mastered the Hemingway way code of courage, endurance and love. He is supposed to excel in the struggle that life must throw on his way. In contrast to this veteran figure, therefore, the forces and ambience of victimization in *The Old Man and the Sea*, Hemingway's most successful and talked about novel, become more prominent and ultimately assume more of a metaphysical nature than those are in a *A Farewell to Arms* or in *For Whom the Bell Tolls*. It is evident, as we shall see, that *The Old Man and the Sea* is more symbolic in its treatment of the protagonist, the locale, and, the action than any other of the Hemingway novels. In steering clear from machines and arms and social issues in *The Old Man and the Sea* Hemingway sticks to the first things of life and in the four days action of the novel dramatizes the existential challenges that man inevitably faces. The sea in the novel is a microcosm which shelters both Santiago and his adversary. It is a source of both sustenance and annihilation. It represents the a moral universe in being merciful and minatory, bountiful and unconcerned, and in offering and withdrawing favor without reason. In containing both the marlin and sharks it embodies the eternal cycle of life and death. Santiago is well aware of the vitality and secret of the sea :

> He always thought of the sea as *la mar* which is what people call her in Spanish when they love her. Sometimes those who love her say bad things of her but they are always said as though she were a woman. Some of the younger fishermen those who used buoys as floats for their lines and had motor-boats, bought when the shark livers had brought much money, spoke of her as *el mar* which is masculine. They spoke of her as a contestant or a place or even an enemy. But the old man always thought of her as feminine and as something that gave or withheld great favors, and if she did wild or wicked things it was because she could not help them. The moon affects her as it does a woman, he thought (Hemingway 1952 : 26-27).

He, however, does not disturb natural harmony by sailing out to the high seas beyond the traditional fishing grounds. In aspiring for a prize catch, not within the can of common mortals, Santiago puts forth a life struggle against unconquerable natural forces in which a kind of victory is possible. When odds are too heavy against him and such victimizing forces as the sense of nothingness, despair, moral conflicts and doubts are bent upon entrapping him Santiago resists defeat with courage, endurance and love. And what is more Santiago not only survives as a victory he also grows in stature as a code hero by gaining greater wisdom and insight into the secret of creation from his lone encounter with marlin and sharks upon the vast, infinite, ongoing reality of the sea.

Before we enter the arena and watch closely the winning struggle of Santiago against his dear foes let us deal shortly with the origin of *The Old Man and the Sea.* Hemingway, after giving vent to his anger and frustration in his novel *Across the River and Into the Trees* (1950) at the aftermath of the Second World War comes once again to take shelter among the simple folks of Cuba. It is here that he writes the tale of the legendary old fisherman Santiago. Before that, in April 1936, Hemingway records the simple outline of the story in an article entitled "on the Blue Water" in the *Esquire* :

> An old man fishing alone in a skiff out of Cabanas hooked a great marlin that on the heavy sash cord hand line pulled the skiff far out to sea. Two days later the old man was picked up by fishermen, 60 miles to the eastward, the head and the forward part of the marlin lashed along side. What was kept of the fish, less than half, weighed 800 pounds. The old man had stayed with him a day, a night while the fish swam deep and pulled the boat up on him and harpooned him. Lashed along side the sharks had hit him and the old man had fought them out alone in the Gulf stream in a skiff, clubbing them stabbing at them, lunging at them with an oar when he was exhausted and the sharks had eaten all they could hold. He was crying in the boat when the fishermen picked him up, half crazy from his loss, and the sharks were still circling the boat (Hemingway 1936 : 184-85).

It is obvious that the idea lies dormant in his mind for a period of about twenty years. And in 1952 he lands his great marlin, *The Old Man and the Sea.*

In developing the character of Santiago, Hemingway attributes many qualities of a real old man, long since dead, who lives in Casablanca on the eastward side of Havana harbor where many commercial fishermen made their headquarters. On 7 February, 1939 he tells Maxwell Perkins of his wish to write the story of the old fisherman. "The book is a fiction," says Hemingway, "based on many actual occurrences." In an interview to *Times* he says, "I tried to make a real old man, a real shark" (Hemingway 1954 : 72).

Extreme old age not withstanding Santiago is, perhaps, the most heroic of Hemingway heroes testing the upper limits of man. He has gone eighty-four days without taking a single fish. He is called "*Salao*", which is the worst form of being unlucky but he does not suffer from any depression. He does not surrender himself to his bad luck by putting an end to his endeavor on the eighty-fourth day. He also does not surrender his independence by going to another boat and sharing other fisherman's luck. He continues his fishing operation alone and takes his failure as an existential challenge. He must accept the challenge no matter what the end brings — success or destruction.

Santiago must sail out into the strange and powerful sea to test man's destiny set against the unconquerable and now unconcerned nature. In their ignorance other fishermen may call him unlucky but so far as the sea is concerned every man is sure to be broken and destroyed. Yet Santiago must set out on his mission to prove that mere destruction is not defeat and that man is a permanent fighter not made for defeat. How, then, does he equip himself for this battle predetermined? As we are told at the very beginning : "He was an old man who fished alone in a skiff in the Gulf Stream and he had gone eighty-four days now without taking a fish" (Hemingway 1952 : 1). His old age, poor health, loneliness added by his long term failure are likely to deepen a sense of despair in the readers. Santiago fishes in a broken skiff whose sail when furled "looked like the flag of permanent defeat" (*ibidem* : 1). Yet the reader need not have to despair. The old man is enriched with wisdom and experience. The tremendous courage he has is his main source of inspiration : "Everything about him was old except his eyes and they were the same color as the sea and were cheerful and undefeated" (*ibidem* : 2). As the Champion fisherman he is well aware of his ability. He suffers from no false humility but is rather ready to prove his mettle once again : "I hope no fish will come along so great that he will prove us wrong" (*ibidem* : 14). The memory of his youth brought back by the recurrent dreams of lions rejuvenates him for the great task ahead. Above all it is the love the old man has for the boy who accepts him as his mentor and godfather that won't allow him to let the boy down. The boy loves and respects Santiago as his idol, the greatest among the fishermen, and for the sake of the boy Santiago cannot bear to break this image of himself. Moreover he wants to work out the example of Dimaggio, the old baseball champion who does "anything perfectly even with the pain of the bone-spur in his heel" (*ibidem* : 66). These are the factors which boosts Santiago's morale to venture out to face squarely the furies that await for him in high seas. To assume that he is a victim of his inordinate aspiration is to miss a vital point. Santiago is no heaven stormer like the mythical Prometheus or the more humanized Ahab of Melvil. He loves his work. He loves to test his potentialities and perfection of skill in the context of existential challenge. It is important to note that in the face of the inevitable destruction Santiago makes the fateful decision of sailing out for the marlin.

On the morning of the fishing expedition, Manalo, the boy, arranges the simple breakfast of Coffee. On the previous night he brings Santiago a supper of black beans and rice, fried bananas, stew and two bottles of beer. The boy won't have the old man fish without eating while he is alive. It is on the eighty-fifth day of Santiago's being a "*Salao*" the boy sees him off into the sea. The boy wishes the old man good luck after helping him launch the skiff.

In catching the big fish and fighting with the sharks, says Carlos Baker, "the gallantry of Santiago is defined in parts by the gallantry of his adversary" (1952 : 296). When the old man feels for the first time the slight nibbling on his line, he at once knows that something is in the offing. Marline is eating the sardine below six hundred feet in the darkness. The huge fish swims off with the bait in his mouth. After four hours the fish is still swimming steadily. Like other Hemingway protagonists, Santiago is trying "not to think but only to endure." He only needs to know what he has against him. Towards midnight Santiago knows that he and his adversary are "joined together and have been since noon and no one to help either of us" (Hemingway 1952 : 55). He cannot apprehend what their fight implies or what waits for them. But all the possibilities of suffering can be smelled easily. He is to pass through phases of suffering in order to prove his courage and endurance.

Near the noon of the second day the great fish surfaces. It is two feet longer than the skiff and obviously no less powerful than the Champion fisherman. Here, one may point out, is a suggestion of victimization when the old man is pushed to the limit and pitted against heavy and nearly insurmountable odds out in the unknown waters of the sea. But Santiago is, in fact, Hemingway's code hero well versed in courage and endurance and hence eligible to be released from the trap of victimization and to achieve the dignity of a victor. The boat is towed for about forty-eight hours and the old man can hardly afford to relax the pull of the line. His hands are cut, he has no sleep and has survived on raw fish and a bottle of water. Yet pain does not matter to him. A parallel situation is noticed in Hemingway's *The Undefeated* where Mannel is shown charging at the bull six times with a broken wrist. The qualities of a victor become yet more formidable in Santiago when he rises beyond his physical pain and the immediate concern of killing the Marlin to realize a kinship and interdependence with the objects of nature. Who could but a victor marvel, in the thick of danger, at the size, strength, beauty, endurance and nobility of the Marlin, his adversary? The sight of the fish inspires the old man to achieve the goal he has set himself for. He is resolute now to prove himself against this worthy adversary : "Let him think I am more man than I am, and I will do so... I will show him what a man can do and what a man endures" (*ibidem* : 67).

Before the fish starts circling on the third day Santiago cannot see clearly. During the night he is frightened, but assures himself : "You better be fearless and confident old man" (*ibidem* : 103). And when the fish finally begins to circle he pierces the harpoon into its heart. Santiago wins the battle but his painful ordeal is not yet over. He has already learned how to suffer and endure. So when the sharks come he is but little perturbed. In his fight with the sharks the old man suffers to the extreme. He loses his harpoon in killing the sharks. His hands are cut in the process. When sharks come in packs he breaks his knife and loses his improvised harpoon in fighting them. He strikes at everything that is visible in the darkness. The sharks eat away the marlin and the old man sails on ignoring them. He behaves perfectly and honorably while losing his prize catch to the sharks. Nothing is left for the sharks at the end of his home bound journey and he is wounded in his chest.

Santiago's fight against the sharks is a nightmare. Yet he wants to carry the spoils of his victory to the shores of civilization. He has firm faith that Manolin would believe him. In his fight with the marlin and the sharks the old man is completely destroyed. At the end of the great expedition, before the dawn of the fourth day, Santiago stands on the rock alone, wounded and exhausted. Shouldering the mast he climbs the hill and reaches his shack to sleep on his bed of newspapers : His mission done the old man feels contented and assured that life would be easier now with Manolin. After all, he is not so unlucky and can leave his legacy with pride and satisfaction. He becomes an object lesson for Manolin who could learn how to fight against odds with courage, determination, endurance, and, at the same time, love for the adversary. Man can only be a victor, as *The Old Man and the Sea* establishes through the struggle of Santiago, when he faces the challenges of life with courage in his heart, smile on his lips and compassion for his fellow beings.

Santiago is the product of Hemingway's search for completeness which has begun with Nick Adams. Nick is a symbol of the twentieth-century disillusionment. He appears, under different names, in Hemingway's novels and reflect the shocked sensibility of modern man. Through various characters and over the space of years Nick grows in stature to ultimately assume the spiritual potentiality of Santiago. Unlike other Hemingway characters, therefore, he needs not pass through the grueling phases of victimization, of suffering and endurance, to attain enlightenment. But, in the interest of the readers, it becomes an authorial responsibility to let Santiago stalk through the harrowing moments of the existential challenge he is made to encounter. Santiago, as his treatment in the novel testifies, is never a victim in the sense Job, Fausts, Oedipus or Ahab, to take some of the prototypes of victims leaving aside the protagonists of the novels examined so far, are victims. Victim-hood inevitably carries with it a sense of deprivation, loss, anger and spite — a sense of being double crossed in one's ignorance or impotence. Santiago, on the contrary, never shows up that he is sold out. Although terribly exhausted in body he never feels lost or desperate. In the moments of worst challenges the memory of lions, the instance of the skillful Dimaggio and his love for the boy make him endure his suffering admirably. Hence we never see him losing temper or cursing. His equanimity of spirit stands him in good stead althroughout. Santiago is never victimized; only we the readers are taken into the high seas to partake the cosmic drama with him. The old man knows that getting killed is as much a part of the code of living as chasing the adversary. The question of being defeated, therefore, does not arise. Even while playing a losing game he is convinced that it is a game all the same. Hence the absence of the spiritual agony that we find in a victim, and, hence the old man's endearing conversation with the birds and the fish he must kill in order to live. He might go on and on into the ocean till eternity itself is folded up but would never feel broken. For it is all the same for him as having a sleep on his bed of old newspapers — living as he exists.

Unlike the celebrated victims in recorded literature, he does not throw up his arms into the unanswering void and cry : cursed be the day when his mother conceived him. Nor does he cry revenge against the ultimate thing that has undone him. Santiago, like the enlightened *rishis* of ancient India, has the key to the secrets of the creation. Before him opens the hidden gates of the domain where cohabit the opposing forces. For him the killer and the killed, the prey and the predator, the stability of the land and the uncertainty of the unknown ocean all become same — elements of the cosmic drama. Thus he could sail on — without calling help from hope — talking to his cramps, birds, little sardins and the big marlin that enjoys running away with him — all calm and composed just as he used to share beer with the boy, little irritated by the others' talk about his being luckless. Quite the same equanimity of spirit later possesses him when he drops the skeleton of the big marlin and struggles up the shore to home and to rest — perhaps never looking back to assess how much gained or lost. It is left to the crowd to wonder. Santiago is never entrapped which is a precondition to victim-hood. For he knows what he does and never gives life a chance to catch him on the wrong foot. In his enlightenment Santiago moves beyond the polarities of victory or victimization to become a *Karmayogi* par excellence.

Thus, as the foregoing analysis of some of the Hemingway heroes underlines, there is a certain pattern of the journey of the Hemingway hero from existential victim-hood, through suffering, endurance and love, to the ultimate victory, albeit on a metaphysical plane. He is made to struggle, which is rather a game of survival, against *nada* presenting itself before him in different forms of "commitment" according his social standing. Although the outcome of the contest is predetermined, the killed or maimed hero attains the winner's berth. And in Hemingway "winners take nothing" except the satisfaction of having learned the "code", to have been able to live or die gracefully in an "age of defeat."

## WORKS CITED

Baker, Carlos, *Ernest Hemingway : Critiques of Four Major Novels*. New York : Charles Scribner's Sons, 1962.

Fiedlier, Leslie A., *Waiting for the End*. London : Jonathan Cape, 1964.

Hemingway, Ernest, *In Our Time*. New York : Charles Scribner's Sons, 1925.

——, *The Sun Also Rises*. New York : Charles Scribner's Sons, 1926.

——, *A Farewell to Arms*. New York : Charles Scribner's Sons, 1929.

——, *To Have and Have Not*. New York : Charles Scribner's Sons, 1937.

——, *The Fifth Columns and First Forty-nine Stories*. New York : Charles Scribner's Sons, 1938.

——, *For Whom the Bell Tolls*. New York : Charles Scribner's Sons, 1940.

——, *Across the River and Into the Trees*. New York : Charles Scribner's Sons, 1950.

——, *The Old Man and the Sea*. New York : Charles Scribner's Sons, 1952.

Howard Milton, "Hemingway and Heroism," *Masses and Mainstream* 5 (Oct. 1952) : 1-8.

Rovit, Earl, *Ernest Hemingway*. New York : Twayne Publishers, 1963.

Sanderson, Stewart, *Hemingway*. Writers and Critics Series. London : Loliver and Boyd, 1961.

Tripathy, B.K., *Osiris N. : The Victim and the American Novel*. Amsterdam : B.R. Gruner Publishing Co., 1985.

Young, Philip, *Ernest Hemingway : A Reconsideration*. New York : Harcourt, Brace and World, 1966.

——, "Ernest Hemingway", *Modern American Novelists*. New York : American Library (1959, 1964) : 146-177.

# 11

# Earnest Hemingway's *The Old Man and the Sea* : A Philosophical Discourse upon the Affirmation and Adventure

*—Gajendra Kumar*

*THE OLD Man and the Sea* — a tour de force in the American fictional world is considered to be a treatise upon affirmation which professes a definite departure from Hemingway's previous literary views and theories. This novel is not of paramount importance for its disillusionment and negation as we locate in other works of art. Santiago cannot be treated as a mentally wounded protagonist as was Jake Barnes in *The Sun Also Rises*; and Lieutenant Henry in *A Farewell to Arms*. This novel proves to be a monumental work in the historiography of the twentieth century American fiction writing in which the struggle for existence and progression has been explored. The human struggle becomes the bone and blood for the survival of the fittest which constitutes the crux of this *magnum opus* work. The novel appears to be a modern edition of the ancient epics which perceives the odds and obstacles of life in a challenging mood. The novel captures the heroic spirit of the Greek tragedies and men who launch their crusade against destiny and succeed in resolving the moral crisis. The protagonist may fail and fall but he achieves a remarkable stature by his titanic resistance. The texture of the novel has been structured around the two heterogeneous approaches and attitudes. On the one hand the novel portrays the social amity and amicability and on the other hand Santiago, the fatherly figure who commands Kudos by getting himself dependent on the restaurant — owner and the wineshop owner. The author himself fits well in the character of Santiago and advocates the contemporary ethos of the American society. Michael Greenberg rightly observes :

> "Earnest Hemingway is one of the leading characters in the story of the American century. From the cultural point of view, he may be the main character. He had a genius for presenting Americans as they wished to be seen, at a time when they were not sure how to see themselves" (X).

The novelist weaves the character of the hero which also suits to his own temperament and taste. To the protagonist even the baseball champion, Joe DiMaggio is unavoidable. From sociological point of view, the novel seems to be a lively documentation of human isolation which focuses the culmination of Hemingway's disinterestedness in the social traffic of life and getting into natural orbit. This is not due to the escapist urge of Santiago rather he has a bubbling desire to get himself liberated. Philosophically the novel becomes a journey from social life to natural life. Quite naturally, even the lost world has its own dictum and disciplines. In Hemingway's literary universe Santiago is the maiden hero who does not come from America and he too is not busy like bee with the modern ethics. In the given situation of the novel, Hemingway deserves to be compared with Joseph Conrad. The novelist because of the new kind of literary adventurism manifests the liberation of the human spirit from the shackles of society and executes Santiago's solitary drama in the very lap of nature. This is a memorable work not because it is the greatest work of Hemingway rather he enunciates the existential philosophy in a very idiosyncratic manner that is individual heroism and reverence for life's struggle. The story is carved out in such a way that it becomes the dynamo of compelling power and persuasion. In the ultimate analysis of the novel, Hemingway does not get himself lost albeit he feels homely, ease and enthusiastic. Owing to the accidental cruelty of the destiny

Hemingway's universe breaks and crucifies a gentleman but there emerges a man who survives and marches ahead like Santiago.

In the pattern of Huck Finn in his 'Adventures' or Jake Barnes in *The Sun Also Rises*, Santiago is alienated from the mainstream of the society because he is *salao*, a very unlucky who did not catch any fish for eighty-four days. The society in which Santiago is born, if one proves to be unlucky, that is treated as something against of the established norms of the community. But in course of time, Santiago makes it clear that he has still the immense power to perform a heroic task which restores his credit and credulity in his own community. In the American tradition of narrative art, we get a number of writers who weave their protagonists according to the demand and desire of the natural environment. In the annals of the tradition Santiago has been chiselled with the novelty and sobriety who derives much pleasure and profit in his intimate relationship with the sea. But in his narratology, Hemingway is not a replica of his predecessors. Firstly he shows his revolutionary fervour while he selects the hero by crossing the border. K.S. House rightly analyses literary relevance of his narrative art :

> In America each individual must find his own way of dealing with chaos. Yet at the end of the nineteenth century a coherent mythology and recognizable attitudes had emerged so that twentieth century writers have been able to analyse, interpret and modify.

Hemingway's interpretation and description gives us a very realistic and titillating account. In his creative discourse, characters are not merely phantoms rather they are blood and flesh of his vision and imagination. Like Thoreau, Twain and Faulkner, Hemingway also celebrates pristine closeness with nature in order to decodify the inherent spiritual urge. Hemingway's Nature is very akin to Wordsworth which is not callous and vindictive as we find in Thomas Hardy. Santiago enjoys ecstasy in the surroundings of the birds and creatures of the sea. Santiago addresses the giant marlin as his friend and brother, the stars are distant friends. The author's account of Santiago's intimacy with Nature and its object reminds Thoreau's relationship with the world of Walden, not Melville's portrait of the sinister and treacherous sea. Being a classic it does not achieve the excellences of other British or American classics.

In its design and description the novel by sustaining classic pace emerges as a didactic novel but its didacticism can be located in various perspectives. The novel lays remarkable emphasis on what men can do, and it lays rather more stress on the world as a battle-field where heroic deeds are possible. The novelist's universe which was full of old fishermen that was not free from pain and problem. But here the message of affirmation is quite in sharp contrast with other works of art like *The Sun Also Rises* and *A Farewell to Arms*. No doubt, one of the important aspects of this universe is its changelessness. Nature is very much sticked to the same rhythm and the same routine. This is the universe where God has very limited role to play. Santiago's character bears the impact of religion as well as superstition. But his views are not relevant to his tragic experience with the great marlin. In this peculiar set up, everyone, changeless and Godless has decided role to play. Santiago is also meant for pursuing marlin. That is the sole mission of his life. Both Santiago and marlin struggle to the last but without any animosity or ill will. The marlin's desire is to dwell in the deepest parts of the sea and escape the pursuit of man. The Old Man has a deep sympathetic affection and all love for the fish. He appreciates its potency and recognises its nobility. In the crucial battle with his hands bleeding and his body utterly exhausted, the Old Man says that the fish is killing him but that it has all right to do so. "Come and Kill me", he says to the marlin. "I do not care who kills who." On his coming back to homeward, the Old Man establishes his final rapport with the fish. He concedes this fact that he does not kill the fish only to keep alive and to sell its meat. He killed it for pride because he is a fisherman. He loved it when it was alive and he loved it after. If he loves it, it was not a sin to kill it.

In a philosophical framework it can be argued that it is a world in which everyone is killing or being killed. Despite this, a sense of brotherhood and love binds together the creatures of Nature, establishing between them a harmony and an emotion which transcends the destructive pattern in which they are caught. Each living thing, man and animal, acts out its destiny according to the compulsion of its nature and in the process becomes a part of the profound integrity of the natural universe. This integrity takes into account the hard facts of pursuit, violence and death, but it reaches a stage of feeling beyond them. Hemingway's philosophy of the universe has this harmony as its fundamental concept. Even the sharks have their own place and position. The sharks are horrible, but the most powerful and the strongest among them, the great Mako Shark, shares the grandeur of the marlin. In the life and death struggle, Santiago kills this shark and feels identified with it also. This shark was not a scavenger nor just "a moving appetite as some sharks are." It was beautiful, noble and fearless. Nature has not only its own harmony and integration but also its degrees of values. There are actually two sets of values in every creatures : the great marlins and the lesser ones, the great sharks and the smaller. In Hemingway's literary contour and nuances, there are also two kinds of men — the greater men, and the lesser heroes and ordinary persons. The literary spectrum of Hemingway covers a wider dimension where current and cross current views jumble and juxtapose because of his stylistic unison of the thing. Janet Wilson rightly analyses the American mode of visualising life and interpreting the general philosophy of life. He says :

> The American artist's concern to depict the two primary experiences of that Autochthonous questing man who is the characteristic American, and the feeling that man is forever a stranger and alone is distinctly evident in most twentieth century writers.... In deceptively simple style, he uses the non-human universe to gain further understanding of the complex, unplumbed depths of the

> human psyche, and the endless surprises encountered in life's journey of what man achieve and endure (32).

Santiago's heroic elements are very dynamic and daring as a protagonist of the novel. He justifies the concept of Aristotelian hero who believes in fight to finish for the noble causes. To be a hero means to expose oneself to greater dangers, to take more risks of defeat and death. Santiago in order to catch a great fish goes beyond the customary fishing area. The fish is so powerful that it pulls his boat even farther out, so far away from the shore that he cannot get back in time to prevent the marlin being consumed by the sharks. The inevitable loss is bound up with the great experience. Nature provides boundless opportunities for the great experience if a human being has the pluck to accept the challenge. The experience carries with it its heavy tragic, but the experience is worth the price. The next day the other fishermen gaze in awe at the size of the skeleton. The usual reverential feeling of the boy Manolin for Santiago is further reinforced. Everyone has somehow been uplifted by the experience. Even the ignorant tourists are struck by a sense of the extraordinary.

The world not only consists in the possibilities of heroic verve and vitality rather it has also continuity. Santiago is extremely old and will not survive very long now. But he has been training Manolin to pick up where he leaves off. The teacher — taught bond between them suggests that the heroic instinct is a part of a continuing process which passes from one generation to another. The universe is thus an endless series of possibilities and affirmations. The philosophical discourse upon affirmation which was subdued in Hemingway's previous novels is sounded here with great confidence and without any sense of doubt. Santiago appears to be the most obvious and organised representation of the hero in the entire gamut of Hemingway's fiction. Santiago is uncommon in the sense that he has not been permanently defeated or disillusioned. His heroic stature is suggested and subscribed everywhere. He emerged as 'the champion' just by defeating a huge Negro at a hand-wrestling match. Now in the last stage of his life he becomes hero worshipped by Manolin. While he was busy in everyday business he usually thinks of Joe DiMaggio, the superstar of baseball of his generation and surprises if DiMaggio, suffering from as bone-spur in his heel, ever endured the pain which the marlin is causing him. And at night when he goes to bed, he dreams of lions playing on the beaches of Africa. The regular association with the king of baseball players and the king of beasts adds to the Old Man's heroic proportions. He is heroic and titanic even in his dooms day and bad fortune. This is the apex of his heroism that he has been allowed to go for eighty-four days even without having a single fish.

Fundamentally, the theme of the novel has been designed on a real incident of a fisherman who once goes on mission to catch a fish but during the fight he has lost his life. In its original form the novel has been planned under four subtitles like "The Sea in Being" and "Dignity of Man" etc. According to Carlos Baker, the novel albeit a picture of the 'rhythms of nature and of human life' analyses the bitter fact of Human life that 'Winner Takes Nothing' : 'Do Or Die' has always been Santiago's credo and he adheres to it gladly. In Conrad's beautiful coinage, Santiago goes "beyond the boundaries of permitted aspiration" and wins truly Conradian victory. In the philosophic paradigm of 'Ancient Mariner' of Coleridge or Shelly's 'Prometheus', Santiago fights for success, perfection and transcendental bliss. He remains dignified even in the face of a great failure. In his work-ethics he is no less diligent than Wordsworth's Leech gatherer.

> "Employment hazardous and wearisome!
> And he had many hardships to endure,
> From pond to pond he roamed, from moor to moor;
> Housing, with God's good help, by choice or chance,
> And in this way he gained an honest maintenance" (196).

Hemingway's leitmotif in this novel is to heighten and intensify the heroic effects that he produces by various means. The extraordinary beauty of Nature fascinates everybody. The account of the sea coming to life at dawn is one of the most moving passages, in the story, supplemented later by the drama of the great pursuit. This culminates into climax with the first great jump of the marlin, when for the first time, Santiago evinces the gigantic size of his prey. Hemingway pays very close attention to the rippling and fluting of the water, to wind currents, to the movements of turtles, porpoise, flying fish, the birds, to the rising of the Sun and the stars. We are filled not simply with a sense of Nature's vastness, but of her enchantment. This enchantment adds an aesthetic dimension to Santiago's adventure. The universe which Hemingway presents and portrays, it is not adequate to have will-power. Once must also know the methods and modes of one's trade. On the practical plane, will-power is what enables a man to survive and technique is what enables a man to be successful. Santiago is a superb craftsman who knows his business thoroughly and always practices it with great skill. He keeps his life line straight where others permit him to drift with the current. Life is not just an endurance contest. It is also an art with rules, rituals and methods that can lead to mastery.

In the general drama of life when the testing time comes the individual becomes solitary. The pull and pressure cannot be shared or passed on to others. Santiago in a pitiable posture with his hands bleeding, his face cut, his body racked with pain and exhaustion wishes time without number that the boy were with him to abate the strain but in the moment of crisis it is necessary that he should go unaccompanied. He must trust upon his own resources and endure his trial unaided. In the battle between individual, man and the natural world, there exists the probability for an individual to rise to his highest level. This work has his own universe which has been recovered from the big wounds that made it so frightening a place in Hemingway's early stories. That world now recaptures its equilibrium in this novel. Actually, the world is no longer a trap in which man is doomed to struggle, to suffer and to die as bravely as he can. The world is, now, located in a meaningful, integrated, and purposive space which challenges human resources and offers rewards and reverence to those who accept it daringly and delightfully. There is no less intensity of cathartic effect but the tragedy has, now, lost its bleakness and accidentality and become object-oriented. It is this attitude of objectivity which substantiates Hemingway's philosophy and makes *The Old Man and the Sea*, a milestone work.

*The Old Man and the Sea* is the climax of Hemingway's prolonged discovery for engagement from the social world and complete entry into the natural. The time to come out of society and its artificial life is prompted not by the intention to escape but the will for liberation. Hemingway desires not to gloss over responsibilities but to liberate his moral and spiritual self. No doubt, the social life has become artificial, cowardice persists not in violating it — but in continuing in it. In order to be justifiable, it is palatable to make a return to thc lost world of Nature. That lost world as the novel exposes has its own liabilities, disciplines, moralities and meanings. The human contact between individualism and interdependence has been one of the vital concerns of the novelist's literary commitment. The novel very clearly and cogently evinces that life cannot be imagined without a realisation of solidarity and inter-dependence. In his venture to search and to catch his big fish, Santiago obtains a deepened moral vision into his ownself and into his contact with the rest of created life. Santiago comes to seek his intimate love for the creature that he himself hunts and kills. He feels the immediacy to overcome this huge fish not simply for his earthly requirement but even more for his pride and his profession.

The great marlin is not identical to the other fish which the Old Man catches so to him the marlin becomes spiritual more than a physical necessity. The marlin is very much prudent for the Old Man, and in course of time Santiago comes to pity, and then to reverence and finally to love. Ultimately, Santiago resolves his crisis that there can be no victory for either in the equal fight between them. Owing to the pull and pressure of the circumstances both of them become one. Albeit the Old Man captures the horrible fish but he came to treat it as his equal and his brother. He enjoys with it a life which is awesome fusion of beauty and violence and where all creatures are both hunter and hunted.

Santiago, right from the beginning to the end, is imbued with heroic wisdoms. He struggles the great fish with epic skill and experience. "A man can be destroyed but not defeated" he says in course of his life-death, struggle with sharks. Here something is above than Santiago's heroic individualism and above than the love and brotherliness what he comes to realise for the marlin, there is an another dimension to the Old Man's realisation. In course of capturing and killing the memorable marlin and in losing it to the sharks, the Old Man comes to know the sin into which individuals fall by going far out beyond their depth or beyond their true place in life. In the beginning of his fight, he felt loneliness and came under the grip of guilt for the way in which he has caught it. After the triumph over the marlin, he does not have the sense of victory or a pride of superiority. The Shark episode does not seem to be accidental rather Santiago has been expecting it as a punishment. The arrival of the Sharks is not an incident of chance or bad luck. It is a straight consequence of the Old Man's effort in killing the fish, the smell of whose blood attracts the fierce killers. In the process of winning and killing the marlin, the Old Man comes in the trap of the eventuality of events and sequences which snatches the fish from him when Santiago begins to love and identify himself with his prey.

Before resolving the problem to capture marlin, Santiago had been jubilant because, "we do not have to try to kill the stars. It was enough to have to kill our fellow creatures." The attack of the sharks gives him an impression that for him the adventure to kill the star prey is "to kill the Sun or the Moon or the stars." To Santiago, simply it was enough to live on the sea and kill "our true brothers." In his individualism and his pride, he went far out "beyond all people, beyond his true place in the world. By doing so he brought on himself as well as on the fish, the forces of violence and destruction. The Old Man's realisation finally leads him to express his regret to the dead fish : "I'm sorry, fish." This realisation and its implications are emphasised symbolically throughout the novel. From the beginning to the end, the theme of solidarity and interdependence pervades the action. Thematically it provides the beautiful paradigm of the story within which the Old Man's heroic individualism and his love for his fellow-creatures appear and act. His eighty-four days have passed without any result, Santiago has become dependent upon the young boy Manolin, and upon his other friends in the village. The boy keeps up his confidence and hope, carries his day to day material for use and observed that he has fresh bait for his fishing. Lastly when he tells himself that fishing kills him exactly as it keeps him alive, he calculates that it is not the fishing only but the love and care of another human being that sustains his life force. "The boy keeps me alive, he thought."

Gradually the Sharks take out more flesh from the great marlin's body and as the boat comes closer to the sea-shore, the Old Man becomes emotive and sensitive and achieves the heightening of the human relationship. He surprises whether anybody is worrying about him. He comes to locate the boy who will worry, of course : But the boy enjoys his love and care that's why he may not worry much. Decidedly the Company of the boy gives him a thrill and he utters, "how pleasant it was to have someone to talk to instead of speaking only to himself and to the sea." At the present juncture he could not oppose the repeated request of the boy for coming back to his boat and he says nothing else about his further voyage. The mutual understanding and coordination, thus constitute the prime theme of this novel. DiMaggio, the baseball champion has ever been the source of inspiration for the Old Man. Spiritually, crucifixion is another symbol reinforcing the thematic structure of the novel. Even on the level of structure, the image of crucifixion which is employed at the end of the novel correlates Santiago with Christ. All these stylistic devices signify solidarity and interdependence, not isolation or alienation.

In the wider context of all art, literature has an independent and dignified entity of its own. Art survives for its own sake and it satisfies the innate creative instinct of mankind. A perusal of the art suggests that it has social, moral and religious significance. The narrative art of the story broadens our knowledge by adding to our information about the sea and its various creatures and their behaviour-pattern. The novel is full of story-elements in its description of the experiences of the fisherman. The novel also throws the sufficient light on human nature by exposing to us the working of the fisherman's mind in the face of the complex situations in which he finds himself. A close scrutiny of the book reveals that it has three dimensional relevance : Sociological, Ethical and Spiritual apart from its being a personal parable — narrating the protagonist's fight with the complex situation.

No doubt, human isolation is at the nucleus of the novel but the book has a social significance. The opening of the story is squarely confronted with a universe in which man's loneliness is the most prime concern. It has also been argued by a critic that this novel is "the culmination of Hemingway's long search for disengagement from the social world and total entry into the natural." If Santiago is supposed to be lonely, it should not be forgotten that he is profoundly aware of the fact that "no man was ever alone on the sea." If Santiago deserts the mankind, the consciousness of society and his attachment with it are never away of his mind and, at last, he comes back to his village where he finds it pleasant "to have some one to talk to instead of speaking only to himself and to the sea". It has significantly been mentioned that the proper instruction of Hemingway's thoughts and art from the beginning and particularly since 1937 had been a come back to society. The return was meant for not in the sense of any particular social ideology but in the wider context of human interdependence and social commitment. Santiago's reliance on the boy Manolin is by itself enough to demonstrate that the subject of interdependence is at the root of the book. Every new problem reminds Manolin's significance. No critical approach can turn down the spiritual bond that is palpable between the Old Man and Manolin. Quite visibly, the novel upholds the concept of solidarity and the need for social bond.

The novel also suggests certain vital moral ethics and ethos. Symbolically, the novel depicts "the theme of the undefeated." Santiago typifies the mental framework of the human being which nullifies all difficulties and stays fearless in the face of all troubles and traumas. This story is praiseworthy for "its stress on what man can do and on the world as an arena where heroic deeds are possible."

Santiago may have been lost to the Sharks but he has won a moral battle by virtue of the heroic struggle that he has fought against them. Defeat or despair cannot suppress the Old Man or lead him to a state of despondency. The philosophic spectrum of the novel focuses the essential invincibility of a human spirit. Apart from human endurance for suffering there are other faculties which come to forefront in the indepth analysis of the novel. Santiago's charity and modesty emanate from a human urge that he and all natural creatures participate in the same pattern of necessity. His politeness and kindness are inextricably mated with his heroism which make Santiago a noble and most respected person.

Hemingway, nowhere, expresses his utmost belief in the benevolence of God. Santiago does not fundamentally appear to be a man of orthodox character. Hemingway shows what he knows from his personal experiences and he transmits it as honestly, directly and cogently as he can. His contribution is not so big as contemporaries have contributed. His area of interest is altogether different in the sense that he has not written on very usual themes and contexts rather he has discussed the full length ideas related to shooting, hunting, fishing, fighting and physical punishment in war, road and air accidents. No doubt, his literary horizon is not wide extensive but he has articulated the themes of the central experiences of his own generation. In his literary purview there comes the voice of the age like war and violence, traditional-values and strain and the meaning of existence. In order to focus this kind of attitude he shows his fervent mood and mind set — with affirmation and the philosophy of survival.

The novelist seeks a co-ordination between the talent and training of the artist and the sportsman. William Faulkner is of the opinion that *The Old Man and the Sea* is 'his best' and 'the best single piece of any of us' which has reasonably drawn critical attention over the decades since its publication in 1952.

## WORKS CITED

Greenberg ,Michael, "Fearing Fear Itself" *The Hindus*, 1 August, 1999.

House, Kay S., 'Foreword', *Reality and Myth in American Literature*, Greenwich, Conn : Fawcett Publications, 1966.

Janet Wilson in "Crossing Borders : Earnest Hemingway's *The Old Man and the Sea* in *Literary Anthropological Folkoristic Perspectives, Modern American Literature*. Ed. Rajeshwar Mittapalli and Claudio Gorlier. New Delhi : The Atlantic Pub., 2001.

Wordsworth, "Resolution and Independence", *The Works of William Wordsworth*. Hertfordshire : Wordsworth Editions Ltd., 1994.

# 12

## *The Old Man and the Sea* : An Archetypal Perspective

*—Mohit K. Ray*

IN *THE Old Man and the Sea*, which is quite different from the other novels by Hemingway in subject and treatment, one finds an age-old archetypal theme adopted in the modern context. What appears significant is the appeal of the novel across space and culture gaps, how it seems to carry a familiar ring to the readers all over the world. This has been possible because of the writer's use of an archetype in this novel which may have its origin in the pre-historic times. This is what largely accounts for the universality of the appeal of this simple, brief, apparently monotonous story of an old fisherman following his fish for three days at a stretch, and coming back at last without achieving any material gain.

The old man, with his small skiff and oars, hooks and harpoon, broken knife and tattered sail, does his fishing like the fishermen of the ancient days, unaided by modern technology. He is too poor to take advantage of motor-boats, ice-crates and the kind of equipments that are used by moneyed tradesmen. He still leads an almost primitive, pre-industrial life on the sea. Consequently, his engagement with his fish is direct, desperate, it seems to be a matter of life-and-death with him. But he does not show or feel any hostility toward his target. Rather he responds to it with a fine sensitiveness. Not only does he sympathise with the fish; he also exhibits a definite respect for it. He has got to kill it. It is his professional compulsion. At the same time he is sorry that he has to kill such a beautiful dignified noble creature. The old man also feels an overflowing love for the smaller fishes, the tortoise, the porpoise, the delicate sea-birds, even the sea itself, which he imagines as a feminine spirit.

A perceptive reader could catch in this text echoes or resonances from the folklores of various fishing communities in different parts of the world. In the coastal areas or on the riverbanks where people had to depend for their livelihood on fishing or hunting, one could still encounter a similar approach to nature; in this life the hunted creature itself becomes part of the great mythicized world of nature, and assumes the same quality of mystery, awesomeness in the hunter's imagination as the sea or river or forest in which it dwells.

In *The Old Man and the Sea* Hemingway stages his own journey as a writer "far out to past" (Nobel Prize speech)[1] as he places his old man in a long line of ancient hunters/fishers, whose wonder, humility, admiration and respect for both the animate and the inanimate worlds around them remained embedded in the collective memory of the race.

As man's earliest occupation, the act of hunting had left its powerful impact on his imagination. The earliest paintings, sagas, legends are about hunting. Many of the early gods/goddesses were imagined and worshipped in the form of hunters or huntresses. Thus hunting, originally a necessity, came to be coloured by creative imagination, and got accommodated in the racial memory and the folklores as myths and archetypes.

The primitive man perceived hunting as a real challenge, a game between equals. This was logically followed by his perception of the victim as a dignified being, even a mysterious spirit, worth deifying. In Frazer one finds the description of the practice of fish worship among certain primitive tribes, who lived largely on fish in their seas and rivers and who performed certain rites on the eve of the fishing season and prayed to the fish to come (18). Frazer also stresses the observance of rules regarding abstinence and purification among the hunters and fishermen of some savage tribes, which were the same rules as applied to manslayers. This shows the status of the killed creature in their perception; it is equal to that of the slayer, *i.e.,* the man, if not higher. Frazer claims : "the savage commonly conceives animals to be endowed with souls and intelligences like his own, and hence he naturally treats them with similar respect" (217).

The way Santiago perceives his fish may find clear parallel in these lores. He talks to his fish as if it were an equal, a human listener. "If you are not tired, fish...you must be very strange" (73). Thus he would go on talking intermittently and intimately till the end. It is, as it were, a friend, a brother, an assistant, with whom communication is possible. "How do you feel fish", the lonely man would ask over the silent see," "...I feel good...pull the boat fish" (78). And later in his state of utter exhaustion he would cry out to the same victim : "Fish,...fish, you are going to have to die any way. Do you have to kill me too?" (90)

At the same time Santiago is convinced of the extraordinariness of his fish, of the strangeness, which makes it mysterious. "Then when the fish (came)...out of the water...he was sure that there was some great strangeness." And he humbly feels, "there is no one worthy of eating him from the manner of his behaviour and his great dignity" (79). It is the same awe that stirred in the primitive hunter as he became engaged with his hunt. The awe is such that he would even prefer to merge his own human identity into that of the creature. Thus Santiago thinks : "Man is not much beside the great birds and beasts. Still I would rather be that beast down there in the darkness of the sea" (73-74). He also sees it as an extension of his own identity, — a friend, a brother. So even as he continues his struggle with the fish he knows : "I am with a friend." It is not only a friend, but an admirable one, with whom he would have gladly exchanged identities. "I wish I was the fish,...with everything he has against my will and intelligence" (70). Whereas the stars in the sky are envisioned in his mythicizing imagination as "all his distant friends," the fish is seen as a closer dearer "friend" (79). This seemingly paradoxical perception in which the killed one is a friend too, and a venerable one, may be explained only when one remembers the archetype behind it, the ancient hunter *vis-a-vis* his hunt.

Again, it is a paradox that saddens Hemingway's old protagonist. He knows that killing the fish is the compulsion of his job. Yet it seems to him to be a puzzling situation, and he finds it hard to get reconciled to the cruel riddle by which "His choice had been to stay in the deep dark water far out beyond all snares and traps and treacheries. My choice was to go there to find him beyond all people" (61). He knows that he "must kill" his friend (79); and he feels sad at having "to kill our true brothers" (70). He voices this sense of sad compulsion as he says to his victim : "Fish...I love you and respect you very much. But I will kill you dead before this day ends" (63). When he kills it at last, there is no mood of jubilation or triumph. "I am sorry that I killed the fish" (98). "I have killed the fish which is my brother" (92). Such utterances in the tone of simple mournfulness go on like the repeated burthen of a dirge.

The empathy with the killed, again a paradox, is evident. As the tired fish jumps up, to take air, Santiago thinks tenderly : "I must hold his pain where it is....Mine does not matter. I can control mine. But his pain could drive him mad" (88). Even after killing it he feels "we sail like brothers", and "when the fish had been hit (by the sharks) it was as though he himself were hit" (98). This empathy of Santiago is tinged with admiration for "all his greatness and his glory" (72) and with a feeling of helplessness at his own situation as a hunter. He shudders at the conjecture if one had to kill the stars or the moon or the sun. Sadly he admits : "It is enough to live on the sea and kill our true brothers" (79).

As he kills his "true brothers Santiago is instinctively aware of a strange bond binding him with the kills; it is an exclusive and inseparable tie that joins him with his victim : "We are joined together.... And no one to help either one of us!" (61). He is "fast to" the fish, and feels he has no respite from this bondage. "He (the fish) stays down forever. Then I will stay down with him forever" (68).

In course of this prolonged struggle and travel together, there are moments when he does not even care "who kills who" and would not mind who brought him in. "You are killing me, fish, the old man thought. But you have a right to. Never have I seen a greater, or more beautiful, or a calmer or more noble thing than you, brother. Come on and kill me. I don't care, who kills who" (91). Again, as he sails home after the killing, he feels confused : "Who is bringing whom in?" Then he happily surrenders to the illusion : "Let him bring me in if it pleases him. I am only better than him through trickery and he meant no harm" (95).

In this way the novel builds around the archetypal theme of a hunter *vis-a-vis* his hunt, and it is packed with echoes from the racial memory as the hunter pursues and admires, kills and loves, pities and respects his hunt.

An epic pattern has been noted in *The Old Man and the Sea.*[2] Indeed the novel represents the infinitely repeated epic theme of man fighting and enduring amidst a mysterious nature of which his hunt is but a part.

Cassirer claimed : "To mythical and religious feeling nature becomes one great society, the society of life" (110). Moved by a similar feeling, the old man of Hemingway, in course of pursuing his hard life, never ceases to wonder at nature including the sea, the sky, the moon, the small and big creatures in it, and tries to understand it in his simple imaginative loving way as the primitive hunters might have done in the ancient days; and this makes up to a large extent for the extraordinary charm of the book.

Allen Tate had observed in his article on Poe : "The imagination of any power at all often projects deepest assumptions about life in symbols that duplicate without the artist's knowledge, certain meanings the origins of which are sometimes as old as the race" (44). *The Old Man and the Sea* offers a unique illustration of this process at work.

Hemingway invites the reader to share with his old man these primordial impressions and the meanings as old as the race.

## NOTES

1. The past driving a writer "far out to past where he can go out to where no one can help him" (quoted by Sheridan Baker 129).
2. Gilbert Highet says : "It is natural that this should be a plot familiar to his readers. It is an epic pattern" (Excerpt quoted by J. Meyers, *Hemingway : The Critical & Heritage.* London : Routledge & Kegan Paul, 1982).

## WORKS CITED

Baker, S., *Ernest Hemingway.* N.Y. : Holt, Rinehart and Winson, 1967.

Cassirer, Ernest, *An Essay on Man* (1944). N.Y. : 1956.

Frazer, J., *The Golden Bough.* Hertfordshire : Wordsworth Reference, 1993.

Hemingway, E., *The Old Man and the Sea.* New Delhi : Kalyani Publishers, 1994.

Tate, A., "Our Cousin, Mr. Poe" *Poe* (Ed. Robert Regan). N.J. : Prentice-Hall, 1967.

## CONTRIBUTORS

**Gajendra Kumar,** P.G. Department of English, Rajendra College, Jai Prakash University, Chapra, Bihar.

**Vinod Kumar Maheshwari,** Reader, Department of English Studies and Research, Agra College, Agra, Uttar Pradesh.

**Gunjan Agarwal,** Department of English, S.B. Memorial Degree College, Agra, Uttar Pradesh.

**N.B. Masal,** Department of English, Dr. Ghali College, Gadhingloj, Kolhapur, Maharashtra.

**Charu Chandra Mishra,** Assistant Professor, K.G. Arts & Science College. Raigarh, Chhatishgarh.

**Susheela Beniwal,** Lecturer in English, Hindu Girls College, Sonepat, Haryana.

**Mary Mohanty,** Lecturer in English, Government Women's College, Puri, Orissa.

**Rama Kundu,** Professor of English, Burdwan University, Burdwan, West Bengal.

**Ishteyaque Shams,** B.R.A. Bihar University, Bihar.

**Amiya Kumar Patra.**

**Mohit K. Ray,** Professor of English, Burdwan University, Burdwan, West Bengal.